ENDORSEMENTS

"Dr. Waters has written an accessible, sound, and pastoral introduction to the life and theology of the Apostle to the Gentiles. Careful exegesis and theological discernment yield concise but rich expositions of Paul's teaching on sin, salvation, the church, redemptive history, and the future. Each thematic treatment closes with consideration of its relevance to the church's life today, building bridges from Paul's proclamation of Christ and His redemptive achievement into the issues that Christians today confront. This brief study is an excellent way to get acquainted with the persecutor-turned-propagator of Christ's gospel, whom God's Spirit inspired to write more New Testament books than anyone else."

—Dr. Dennis E. Johnson
Professor of practical theology
Westminster Seminary California, Escondido, Calif.

"*The Life and Theology of Paul* is a very useful introductory treatment of the major contours of Paul's theology. While conversant with contemporary scholarship, the author does an excellent job focusing on what is most essential and in distilling complex interpretive issues. Warmly recommended!"

—Dr. Andreas J. Köstenberger
Founder of Biblical Foundations
Senior research professor of New Testament and biblical theology
Southeastern Baptist Theological Seminary, Wake Forest, N.C.

"If you are looking for a concise, clear, and faithful summary of Paul's theology, Guy Waters' work is the perfect fit. Waters faithfully exposits some of the main themes in Paul's thought and also includes practical lessons for believers and churches today. A very helpful resource for students, pastors, and those who are looking for a brief textbook on Paul's theology."

—Dr. Thomas R. Schreiner
James Harrison Buchanan Professor New Testament Interpretation
The Southern Baptist Theological Seminary, Louisville, Ky.

# THE LIFE
# AND THEOLOGY
# OF PAUL

# THE LIFE

# AND THEOLOGY

# OF PAUL

GUY PRENTISS WATERS

ℝ *Reformation Trust*   A DIVISION OF LIGONIER MINISTRIES, ORLANDO, FL

*The Life and Theology of Paul*
© 2017 by Guy Prentiss Waters

Published by Reformation Trust Publishing
A division of Ligonier Ministries
421 Ligonier Court, Sanford, FL 32771
Ligonier.org    ReformationTrust.com

Printed in York, Pennsylvania
Maple Press
December 2017
First edition

ISBN 978-1-56769-865-7 (Hardcover)
ISBN 978-1-56769-880-0 (ePub)
ISBN 978-1-56769-881-7 (Kindle)

Interior design and typeset: Katherine Lloyd, The DESK

Scripture quotations are from the ESV® Bible (The Holy Bible, English Standard Version®), copyright © 2001 by Crossway, a publishing ministry of Good News Publishers. Used by permission. All rights reserved.

Library of Congress Cataloging in Publication Control Number: 2017029688

# CONTENTS

# Chapter 1

---

# INTRODUCTION
# TO PAUL

I t is hard to overstate the influence of the Apostle Paul. One measure of his influence can be seen in that his letters were instrumental in the conversion of three men who would become some of the most important theologians and leaders of the Christian church.[1] In the year 386, Augustine (354–430) found himself weeping beneath a fig tree.[2] He was overwhelmed by a sense of the guilt and power of his sin. At that moment, he heard a child singing a song—*"tolle lege, tolle lege"* (take and read; take and read). Augustine arose and picked up a book containing the Apostle Paul's letters. He read the first words that met his eyes: "Not in sexual immorality and sensuality, not in quarreling and jealousy. But put on the Lord Jesus Christ, and make no provision for the flesh, to gratify its desires" (Rom. 13:13b–14). The effect of these words on Augustine was immediate and powerful. He comments, "For instantly even with the end of this sentence, by a light as it were of confidence now darted into my heart, all the darkness of doubting vanished away."[3] Augustine had been converted.

---

1 Much of the biographical material that follows has been drawn from my "Romans" in *A Biblical-Theological Introduction to the New Testament: The Gospel Realized*, ed. Michael J. Kruger (Wheaton, Ill.: Crossway, 2016), 169–70.

2 Augustine relates the details of his conversion at *Confessions* 8.12, from which the following account is drawn.

3 *Confessions* 8.12, LCL translation.

More than a thousand years later, a German monk named Martin Luther (1483–1546) struggled to find peace of conscience. Luther's years of prayer, fasting, confession, and a pilgrimage to Rome had failed to give him spiritual rest. In 1519, while studying in the Tower of the Black Cloister, Luther came across these words from Paul: "For in [the gospel] the righteousness of God is revealed from faith for faith, as it is written, 'The righteous shall live by faith'" (Rom. 1:17). Luther realized that the righteousness he needed as a sinner was not something that he could merit by his own efforts. This righteousness was the gift of God in the gospel—received through faith, not earned by his works. Once this gospel insight penetrated Luther's soul, he was a changed man: "Here I felt that I was altogether born again and had entered paradise itself through open gates."[4] Neither Martin Luther nor the Western church would be the same again.

In the early eighteenth century, a young Anglican priest pursued the rigors of a strict devotional life and even hazarded a perilous missionary trip to the New World. Despite all of these labors, this priest, John Wesley (1703–91), knew that he was unconverted. It was in 1738, on Aldersgate Street in London, that Wesley underwent a life-changing experience. He attended a gathering where the preface to Martin Luther's commentary on Romans was being read. Wesley commented on what happened to him as he listened: "I felt my heart strangely warmed. I felt I did trust in Christ, Christ alone for salvation; and an assurance was given me that He had taken away my sins, even mine, and saved me from the law of sin and death."[5] The message of Paul's epistle to the Romans, as summarized in Luther's preface, worked in power on Wesley's soul.

## Paul's Influence

The influence of Paul's letters extends well beyond these three towering figures of church history. The entire Christian church is indebted to Paul for much of what we know about the gospel. Without Paul's letters, we would know far less about such precious biblical truths as election, calling,

---

4  Cited in Timothy F. Lull and William R. Russell, eds., *Martin Luther's Basic Theological Writings*, 3rd ed. (Philadelphia: Fortress, 2012), 497.

5  *The Journal of the Rev. John Wesley, A.M. (enlarged from original mss. with notes from unpublished diaries, annotations, maps, and illustrations)*, ed. Nehemiah Curnock (London: Culley, 1909), 1:475–76.

justification, adoption, sanctification, and glorification. Where would the church be without the Apostle Paul?

One cannot think of Paul without a sense of admiration and wonder at the ways in which the Lord Jesus Christ has used him in the lives of God's people. He is one of the greatest minds ever to have graced the Christian church. He is responsible for penning, by inspiration of the Holy Spirit, thirteen of the twenty-seven books of the New Testament. He was a fearless preacher, bringing the gospel of Christ to "the end of the earth" (Acts 1:8). He has left, in the pages of the New Testament, an example that every Christian must follow (1 Cor. 4:16; 11:1).

But this is not the way that the very earliest Christians would have regarded Paul. If you were a Christian believer in Jerusalem a few years after the resurrection of Christ, you probably would have regarded Paul with suspicion and dread. When Paul stepped into the church in Jerusalem and announced that he had become a believer, the "disciples . . . were all afraid of him, for they did not believe that he was a disciple" (Acts 9:26).

Why was Paul so feared by the Christian church in those early days? Paul was feared because he had been a ferocious persecutor of the church. Reflecting on his life in Judaism, Paul told the Galatians that he had "once tried to destroy" the faith (Gal. 1:23), and that he had "persecuted the church of God violently and tried to destroy it" (Gal. 1:13). Paul wanted to exterminate the faith—and all those who embraced that faith.

Luke's account in Acts confirms Paul's testimony. Had Jesus not stopped Paul in his tracks on the road to Damascus, Paul would have followed through on his intent to bring "any belonging to the Way . . . bound to Jerusalem" (Acts 9:2). Paul was not content with seeing Christians arrested. He wanted them dead. "I persecuted this Way to the death" (Acts 22:4); "but when [the disciples] were put to death I cast my vote against them" (Acts 26:10). Not even women were exempt from Paul's persecution (Acts 22:4). Because of Paul, husbands and wives were forcibly separated and children were left without their mothers and fathers.

Paul never forgot this dark chapter of his life. In one of his last letters, writing to a beloved younger colleague in the ministry, Paul reflected on his past:

Formerly I was a blasphemer, persecutor, and insolent opponent. But I received mercy because I had acted ignorantly in unbelief, and

3

the grace of our Lord overflowed for me with the faith and love that are in Christ Jesus. The saying is trustworthy and deserving of full acceptance, that Christ Jesus came into the world to save sinners, of whom I am the foremost. But I received mercy for this reason, that in me, as the foremost, Jesus Christ might display his perfect patience as an example to those who were to believe in him for eternal life. To the King of the ages, immortal, invisible, the only God, be honor and glory forever and ever. Amen. (1 Tim. 1:13–17)

In these autobiographical reflections, Paul testifies to the main themes of his letters. He exemplifies, in the first place, a deep awareness of human sin. Paul is the "foremost" of "sinners," that is, at the front rank of a sinful humanity. Paul points to nothing in himself that would commend him to the saving grace of Jesus Christ.[6] On the contrary, his record merits only judgment and condemnation. Second, he cites the historical reality of Christ Jesus' having come "into the world" in order to "save sinners." As a result, Paul received overflowing "grace" and "mercy" from Jesus. This grace not only rescued Paul from the guilt and bondage of sin, but it also established Paul as an "example" to others—the prototype and pattern of Christ's redemptive work in human beings. Third, Paul emphasizes that the goal of Christ's mission and its redemptive fruit in the lives of sinners is the glory of God (1 Tim. 1:17). God the Father sent Christ into the world to save the undeserving, and Christ accomplished the work of salvation in order to bring glory to the Father. Believers should, in every area of life, strive to declare and show forth the excellencies of the God who both made and redeemed them.

## Paul's Pre-Christian Life

Paul's life was a testimony to the gospel that he preached, so knowing something about his life helps us have a fuller and richer grasp of his message. In

---

6  When Paul says, "I received mercy because I had acted ignorantly in unbelief," he is not pointing to his ignorant unbelief as a meriting or procuring cause of divine mercy. He is likely stressing that his persecuting activity was not an instance of blasphemy against the Holy Spirit (see Mark 3:22–30). To blaspheme the Holy Spirit is to render oneself "guilty of an eternal sin" which God has purposed not to forgive (Mark 3:29). In that respect, Paul had not found himself outside the appointed bounds of God's mercy.

the remainder of this chapter, we will look at what may be said about Paul's life before his conversion. In the next chapter, we will give special attention to Paul's call and conversion.

We have no biography of Paul, whether from his own hand or from someone else's. Paul's thirteen letters and Luke's account of the early church (Acts), however, give us a window into Paul's pre-Christian life. The details in Acts and Paul's letters provide the necessary context for coming to a fuller appreciation of the ministry and message of the Apostle, since many of these details have relevance for our understanding of Paul's Christian life and Apostolic ministry. Nine of these details have special import.

The first concerns Paul's appearance. The New Testament does not provide a physical description of Paul. It does, however, include an indirect comment from his opponents: "For they say, 'His letters are weighty and strong, but his bodily presence is weak, and his speech of no account'" (2 Cor. 10:10). Based on this caricature, Paul does not seem to have been a physically imposing person, and his rhetorical abilities were not well regarded by his opponents. An early but apocryphal second-century description of Paul describes the Apostle as "a man of little stature, thin-haired upon the head, crooked in the legs, of good state in the body, with eyebrows joining and nose somewhat hooked, full of grace."[7]

We do know that Paul undertook his Apostolic ministry in physical infirmity. He appears to have suffered some illness or debilitation when he preached in Galatia (Gal. 4:13). His listing of sufferings for Christ in 2 Corinthians 11:23–29 includes lashings, beatings, and being stoned. His body would surely have borne the marks of this brutal treatment (see Gal. 6:17). No assessment of Paul's ministry, then, may attribute its success to the Apostle's outward appearance. But Paul did not regard this factor as disqualifying him from his Apostolic ministry. On the contrary, he said such "weakness" was a mark of his ministry (see 2 Cor. 10:1–12:21).

The second detail of note concerns the Apostle's name. Attentive readers of the New Testament observe that early in the narrative of Acts, Luke

---

7 Acts of Paul 3, as cited at John McRay, *Paul: His Life and Teaching* (Grand Rapids, Mich.: Baker, 2003), 39.

consistently references the Apostle as "Saul." Beginning in Acts 13:9, Luke consistently references him as "Paul."[8] Why the change in name?

The change is not because "Saul" was Paul's pre-Christian name and "Paul" was his Christian name, as is commonly thought. For a significant portion of Paul's early Christian life, Luke refers to the Apostle as "Saul." Luke gives us a clue concerning the shift, rather, in Acts 13:9 ("But Saul, who was also called Paul"). Paul had both a Jewish name (Saul), and a Roman name (Paul). Paul's Jewish name reflects his descent from the tribe of Benjamin (Phil. 3:5), whose most famous son was King Saul. The name "Paul" was one of three names that he would have received under Roman naming conventions; the other two are lost to history. "Paul" was his *cognomen*, or personal name.[9] The occasion when Paul began to use his Roman name with consistency was a crucial one. It marked the beginnings of the Apostle's labors among largely Gentile populations. In the providence of God, Paul was a man whose names facilitated his ease of movement in both Jewish and Gentile circles.

The third detail of the life and ministry of Paul concerns his heritage. In Philippians 3:5, Paul remarks that he was "circumcised on the eighth day, of the people of Israel, of the tribe of Benjamin, a Hebrew of Hebrews." That Paul was circumcised on the eighth day according to the Mosaic law (see Gen. 17:12) tells us at least that his father was an observant Jew. That he was likely named for King Saul suggests his father's embrace of his own heritage as an Israelite of the tribe of Benjamin. That Paul describes himself as "a Hebrew of Hebrews" tells us that Paul himself embraced his Jewish upbringing and did so with enthusiasm. For all the cultural pressures either to apostasy or to syncretism, Paul consciously remained an observant Jew.

The fourth detail we learn about Paul from his letters and from Acts concerns his family. We have already seen indications that Paul's father was observant of the Mosaic law. We may presume that the family was faithful to worship regularly at their local synagogue and to travel regularly

---

8  Two important exceptions are found in Paul's autobiographical account of his conversion on the Damascus Road before the Jews in Acts 22 and before Agrippa in Acts 26. Here, Paul quotes the words of the risen Jesus as they were spoken to him on that occasion ("Saul, Saul"; see Acts 22:7; 26:14), and the words of Ananias spoken to him shortly afterwards in Damascus ("Brother Saul, receive your sight"; see Acts 22:13).

9  For more on Paul's Roman names and on Roman names in the New Testament, see McRay, *Paul*, 25–28.

to Jerusalem in order to worship at the annual feasts that the Mosaic law required old covenant believers to attend. However, we do not have many specific details about Paul's family members.

We know that Paul's father was a Roman citizen, since Paul was born a Roman citizen and did not acquire his citizenship later in life. We do not know, however, under what circumstances or when Paul's father came by that citizenship. In Acts 23:16 we learn that Paul had a nephew ("the son of Paul's sister") who presumably resided in Jerusalem. Paul, then, had at least one sibling and appears to have been on cordial terms with her. Nowhere in his correspondence does Paul mention a wife or children of his own. At the time that he wrote 1 Corinthians, he was single, and that by God's calling (1 Cor. 7:6–7).[10] It is possible that Paul was a widower, but his marital history remains a matter of speculation.

The fifth significant detail concerns the Apostle's citizenship. Paul, we have noted, was born a Roman citizen. He appeals to his citizenship twice in the course of his Apostolic ministry (Acts 16:37; 22:28). In both cases, Paul invoked his citizenship because Roman officials were depriving him of rights that were his by Roman law. On another occasion, Paul invoked his right as a citizen to have his legal case transferred from the governor, Agrippa, to Emperor Nero (Acts 25:11). This transfer, Luke suggests, likely saved Paul's life (Acts 25:3). In each instance, Paul used his citizenship to prolong his Apostolic preaching ministry and to extend its sphere.

Paul's place of birth is the sixth detail specified by the New Testament. Paul tells us that he was born in "Tarsus in Cilicia" (Acts 22:3). Tarsus was located not far from the Mediterranean coast in what is today southeastern Turkey. It was connected to other major cities by road, and it was an international center of learning. It was no backwater village; it was, in Paul's words, "no obscure city" (Acts 21:39). Like other major Mediterranean cities, Tarsus housed a Jewish community. First-century Jewish communities, while distinct, were not isolated from the other peoples and cultures among whom they lived. As we shall see, Paul himself gives indications of having been raised in a cosmopolitan environment.

---

10 That Paul was not married was not a requirement for the Apostleship, nor is it a requirement to hold office in the church. Neither does Paul view single believers as the spiritual superiors of married believers. See the whole of 1 Corinthians 7 and 1 Corinthians 9:5.

The seventh detail about the life of Paul concerns his education. Paul was a man with a reputation for learning (see Acts 26:24). By his own testimony, he was "brought up in [Jerusalem], educated at the feet of Gamaliel, according to the strict manner of the law of our fathers" (Acts 22:3). Although he was born in Tarsus, Paul received his formal education in Jerusalem, under the tutelage of the noted rabbi Gamaliel (see Acts 5:34). Paul describes himself as a "Pharisee" (Phil. 3:5). The Pharisees were an influential and respected group within Judaism who were committed to upholding both the written law of Moses and the oral law, the body of unwritten traditions that had grown up around the Mosaic law.[11] Identification with the Pharisees set Paul apart, for example, from the Sadducees, who accepted the authority only of the Pentateuch (Genesis–Deuteronomy) and who did not believe in the resurrection from the dead (see Acts 23:6–10). Efforts to situate Paul in one of the competing Pharisaic "schools" in the first century have not proven persuasive. What we do know is that Paul embraced the Pharisaical education that he received and excelled in it. He tells the Galatians that "I was advancing in Judaism beyond many of my own age among my people, so extremely zealous was I for the traditions of my fathers" (Gal. 1:14). Paul, then, sat at the "top of his class" as a young student.

Paul would have received a thorough education in both the Old Testament Scripture and the legal traditions that had grown up in Judaism after and alongside that Scripture (see Gal. 1:14). Paul's frequent citations of the Old Testament suggest that he had committed large portions, if not the entirety, of the Old Testament to memory. In Romans 15:8–13, for example, Paul cites four passages of Scripture (2 Sam. 22:50 [=Ps. 18:49]; Deut. 32:43; Ps. 117:1; Isa. 11:10). What each of these passages has in common is the word *Gentiles*. Since Paul did not have available to him a printed concordance, we are bound to conclude that he accessed these passages from memory.

The New Testament indicates that Paul was conversant in at least four languages. His use of the Old Testament in his letters suggests competence in Hebrew. His letters show that he was fluent in Greek. Luke tells us that he spoke in Aramaic, the language commonly spoken by Jews in Palestine

---

11 The Pharisees were the immediate forebears of the rabbis who, after the temple's destruction in AD 70, would be responsible for transforming first-century Judaism into the Judaism of the medieval and modern eras.

(see Acts 21:40). His travels in the western part of the Roman Empire, and his plans to minister in Spain (see Rom. 15), suggest that Paul was fluent in Latin, the main language of that part of the Roman world.

The New Testament also suggests that Paul was familiar with non-Jewish literature. In Athens, he quotes before the Areopagus the poets Epimenides of Crete (sixth century BC) and Aratus of Cilicia (third century BC) (Acts 17:28; see Titus 1:12). His Areopagus address also evidences awareness of and deft interaction with Stoic and Epicurean philosophy. Paul did not shy away from the study of Greco-Roman literature and thought, and he was not afraid to employ it in service of the gospel.

The eighth fact about Paul revealed in the New Testament is his occupation. Paul was a tentmaker by trade (Acts 18:3), and he likely learned this trade from his father. That a man with extensive formal education should have engaged in manual labor may surprise modern readers, even as it would have scandalized many Greeks and Romans in the ancient world. It was customary, however, for learned Pharisees to earn a living, and many Pharisees worked with their hands.

Tentmakers built and repaired tents, which were in demand among military personnel. Tent making was a portable trade and well suited for an itinerant such as Paul. For Paul, tent making afforded him financial independence from the congregations he served. This independence was important to Paul, who was concerned to distinguish himself from the often financially predatory traveling teachers in antiquity. It was Paul's boast and delight to offer the gospel "free of charge" (1 Cor. 9:18) and to tell his churches that he had "worked night and day, that we might not be a burden to any of you" (1 Thess. 2:9).[12] Paul did so, in part, to substantiate his claims that his ministry was not motivated by greed (Acts 20:33–34) and, in part, to offer a model or example to believers of diligence in a lawful calling (2 Thess. 3:7–9).

The ninth aspect of Paul's pre-Christian life revealed in Acts and the Pauline Epistles made an indelible impact on the Apostle's self-consciousness—his persecution of the Christian church. In Paul's own accounts of his

---

12 Paul insists throughout 1 Corinthians 9, however, that the minister is owed the support of those whom he serves. The Apostle opted not to exercise this right in Corinth, Thessalonica, and other places because the interests of the gospel demanded it.

pre-Christian life in Acts (Acts 22; 26) and in his letters (Gal. 1; 1 Tim. 1), persecution dominates his autobiography. Writing to Timothy, we have seen, Paul could state of his pre-Christian life that he was "formerly . . . a blasphemer, a persecutor, and insolent opponent" (1 Tim. 1:13). That Jesus of Nazareth, who had been deemed a blasphemer by the Jewish leadership and executed for treason by the Romans, should be regarded as Israel's Messiah and worshiped as the Son of God was too much for Saul the Pharisee to bear. Only the risen Lord Jesus Himself could bring Paul's ferocious persecution to a swift and final conclusion.

## Lessons for Today

Paul's pre-Christian biography speaks to the church today in two important ways. First, we see that God, in His providence, was preparing Paul from the womb to be the "Apostle to the Gentiles." God was doing so in ways that Paul could not have foreseen. Paul's place of birth, his heritage, his education, and his vocation were all means by which God was molding and fashioning Paul to be the servant whom God had purposed him to be. All Christians should look back in gratitude to the God who makes and sustains us when we trace the paths by which God has brought us to the places we are now. Reflecting on God's providence in this way helps us renew our trust and confidence in God to lead us into the future even when that future may seem grim and uncertain.

Second, when the saving grace of God transformed Paul's life, it did not make him into someone other than Paul. That is, Paul did not cease to be of Jewish heritage, an educated man, a tentmaker, a citizen, and so on. Grace transformed Paul and brought him under the lordship of Jesus Christ. Whereas these aspects of Paul's life had once been employed in rebellion against Christ, after his conversion they were employed in the service of Christ. We should think about our lives in the same way. As Christians, we have a brand-new relationship with sin and a brand-new relationship with Jesus Christ. Therefore, we should ask how we can use the details and experiences of our lives to advance the glory of the One who loved us and gave Himself for us.

# Chapter 2

---

# THE CONVERSION
# AND CALL OF PAUL

The previous chapter sketched the life of the Apostle Paul up to his conversion on the Damascus Road.[1] We observed that Paul's life bore the trademark of the God who made, sustained, and, in time, redeemed him. The God who had "set [Paul] apart before [he] was born" (Gal. 1:15) was preparing Paul to be the powerful servant of Christ that he would prove to be.

But to be *that* servant, one thing was both needed and lacking—the saving grace of God in Christ. Before his conversion, all of Paul's abilities and accomplishments were put in the service of rebellion against Christ. Paul would need a radical transformation to be a servant of Christ—he would need to be transformed down to the very roots of his being.

That transformation took place on the Damascus Road. Paul's conversion made an indelible mark on his life and memory. He reflects on this experience in three places in his epistles (Gal. 1; Phil. 3; 1 Tim. 1).

---

1 When we speak of Paul's conversion on the Damascus Road, we have in mind what transpired between Paul's being struck blind outside the city of Damascus and Ananias' visit to Paul in the city of Damascus, at which visit "something like scales fell from his eyes, and he regained his sight" (Acts 9:18). It was within that time frame that Paul was regenerated and soundly converted, even if we are unable to pinpoint the precise moment within that time frame when Paul decisively and irreversibly crossed the threshold from spiritual darkness to spiritual light, and then began to exercise for the first time true repentance and saving faith in Christ

The importance of Paul's conversion, however, transcended Paul's person. It was a momentous occasion in the life of the early church, indeed, in the full sweep of redemptive history. The significance of this event for the church is evident in the fact that Luke documents it three times in Acts (chaps. 9; 22; 26). As Luke charts the progress of the gospel from Jerusalem to Judea to Samaria to the end of the earth (Acts 1:8), it is in the ministry of the Apostle Paul that the gospel decisively, triumphantly, and irreversibly crosses the threshold from Jew to Greek. Paul was not the only or even the first person to take the gospel to the Gentiles. He was tasked, however, with overseeing the epochal movement of the gospel to the nations. Paul's conversion, then, was critical to the outworking of God's plan to bring the good news to the end of the earth.

## A True Conversion?

Many readers of Acts have assumed that on the Damascus Road Paul was both called to be the Apostle to the Gentiles and converted by the saving grace of God in Christ. In the last fifty years, however, some New Testament scholars have questioned whether Paul underwent a conversion on the Damascus Road. They argue that Paul did believe himself to have been called to Apostleship. But they question whether Paul experienced a conversion from Judaism to Christianity, from one religion to another.

Some of these scholars have accused Protestants of trying to strain Paul through the eye of the Augustinian/Lutheran needle. As we saw in the previous chapter, Augustine and Luther were men who experienced a profound sense of the guilt of their own sin. Both men found release from that guilt in the gospel they discovered in Scripture, and particularly in the writings of Paul. Some have alleged that Augustine and Luther read their own religious experiences back into Paul and that later interpreters have followed suit. It has been assumed, these critics claim, that Paul had the same religious sensitivity, an "introspective conscience," as these two later Christians.[2] But the evidence, these critics maintain, does not support the conclusion that Paul underwent a conversion in the traditional sense of the word.

---

2 The phrase is that of Krister Stendahl, a twentieth-century critical scholar of the New Testament. Stendahl influentially argued that Paul experienced a call but not a conversion on the Damascus Road.

In reply, we may make two observations. First, we should be clear what we mean and do not mean when we speak of Paul's conversion. We are not saying that Paul necessarily underwent a psychologically dramatic or emotionally charged religious experience. Biblical conversion must not be defined in terms of the subjective phenomena that may sometimes accompany it. Nor are we saying that Paul had spent his life in Judaism burdened by a crushing load of guilt. It is possible that he did, but more likely that he did not (see Phil. 3:6). Rather, we are saying that there came a point in Paul's experience when he was made alive after he had previously been spiritually dead in trespasses and sins. Convinced of his sin and of his helplessness as a sinner, he decisively turned from that sin to Christ in repentance and faith. That moment of transition from spiritual death to spiritual life came on the Damascus Road. That is what we mean by Paul's conversion.

Second, these scholars have unfortunately rent asunder what God has put together. Paul, we will see, was both converted *and* called on the Damascus Road. To separate the two is to distort and misunderstand these features of the Apostle's life and ministry. Paul's conversion and call are two strands of the same cord, inextricably bound and interwoven. Each touches on and leads to the other.

## The Damascus Road Experience

In order to understand the biblical testimony concerning Paul's experience on the road to Damascus, we may ask three questions. First, why was Paul making his way from Jerusalem to Damascus? Luke tells us that Paul was present at and approving of the martyrdom of Stephen (Acts 7:58; 8:1). The sight of the brutal murder of Stephen in no way dampened Paul's persecuting zeal. Stephen's death was immediately followed by "a great persecution against the church in Jerusalem," one that resulted in "all" the saints being "scattered throughout the regions of Judea and Samaria" (Acts 8:1). Saul received official sanction from the Jerusalem authorities to pursue Christians "to the synagogues at Damascus, [to find] any belonging to the Way, men or women" (Acts 9:2). Saul then undertook the long journey from Jerusalem to Damascus.

The second question we may ask about the Damascus Road experience is, what happened to Saul on that journey? Saul had nearly reached

Damascus when two extraordinary things happened—he saw something and he heard something. He first saw a supernatural light: "Suddenly a light from heaven shone around him" (Acts 9:3). It was "about noon" (Acts 22:6), so it was not a natural nighttime occurrence. The light was "brighter than the sun" (Acts 26:13), so Saul did not confuse the light with the sun. Saul and his companions fell to the ground (Acts 26:14), and then Saul also heard a supernatural sound: "Saul, Saul, why are you persecuting me?" (Acts 9:4; 22:7; see 26:14). His fellow travelers heard the sound, even as they had seen the light. But only Saul discerned the voice (Acts 9:7; 22:9).

Saul, now on the ground, discovered that he was blind. His presumably sighted companions had to lead him "by the hand" for the remainder of the journey to Damascus (Acts 9:8). For "three days he was without sight, and neither ate nor drank" (Acts 9:9) until, through the instrumentality of a Christian disciple named Ananias, Saul regained his sight and received Christian baptism (Acts 9:10–19; 22:12–16).

The third question about Paul's experience is, what did the risen Jesus say to Saul on the Damascus Road? Do His words in any way shed light on the experiences that Paul underwent on that occasion? Jesus' commissioning of Saul is recorded in three places in Acts:

> [Saul] is a chosen instrument of mine to carry my name before the Gentiles and kings and the children of Israel. For I will show him how much he must suffer for the sake of my name. (Acts 9:15–16)

> The God of our fathers appointed you to know his will, to see the Righteous One and to hear a voice from his mouth; for you will be a witness for him to everyone of what you have seen and heard. (Acts 22:14–15)

> But rise and stand upon your feet, for I have appeared to you for this purpose, to appoint you as a servant and witness to the things in which you have seen me and to those in which I will appear to you, delivering you from your people and from the Gentiles—to whom I am sending you to open their eyes, so that they may turn from darkness to light and from the power of Satan to God, that they may receive forgiveness of sins and a place among those who are sanctified by faith in me. (Acts 26:16–18)

The first of these accounts contains the words of Jesus to Ananias in Damascus; the second, Ananias' words to Saul in Damascus; the third, Jesus' words to Saul on the Damascus Road.

When we consider these accounts together, we learn two things about Saul's call and conversion: what Jesus called Saul to do and what Jesus would do through Saul. First, we see that Saul was entrusted with bearing Jesus' name to human beings (Acts 9:15). As such, Saul was commissioned as Jesus' "witness" (Acts 22:15), as His "servant and witness" (Acts 26:16). What rendered him competent as Jesus' witness was that he had both seen and heard the risen Jesus (Acts 22:15; 26:16; 1 Cor. 9:1). The sphere of Saul's witness was not only to people in Damascus or Jerusalem. It was to "Gentiles and kings and the children of Israel" (Acts 9:15; see 26:27). Saul would bear witness to all kinds of people, but he had a particular calling to bear witness to Jesus among the Gentiles.

Second, these words of commission tell us that Jesus would undertake a great work in the lives of human beings in conjunction with Saul's bearing witness to Him. Specifically, Jesus would "open their eyes," that is, the eyes of those people before whom Saul bore witness to Jesus. They would "turn from darkness to light" (Acts 26:18), from blindness to sight. Of course, Saul himself underwent the same experience—through Ananias: "Something like scales fell from [Saul's] eyes, and he regained his sight" (Acts 9:18). This experience of having Jesus open one's eyes happens, for both Paul and his hearers, in conjunction with Jesus' word. Saul heard the word of Jesus, was struck blind, and subsequently regained his sight. In like manner, Saul's hearers would hear the word of Jesus through Saul and be brought from blindness to sight.

Saul, then, would serve as a pattern or model of what Jesus Christ would do in the lives of men and women who hear Saul's witness to Christ.[3] We may safely conclude that what Jesus pledged to do in the lives of Saul's hearers, He had already done in the life of Saul.

In Acts 26:18, we receive a glimpse of the work of Jesus Christ in the lives of Saul's hearers and of Saul himself. Jesus, Paul says, "open[s] . . . eyes,

---

3  The testimony of Acts and Paul's own teaching preclude these realities as true of each and every hearer of Paul's gospel. Many of Paul's hearers remained culpably in darkness and unbelief. The Word is the occasion of the exercise of God's saving power toward only those whom God has eternally and unchangeably purposed to save (see Eph. 1:1–11).

so that [people] may turn from darkness to light." One purpose of opening people's eyes is so that they may be brought from "darkness" to "light." In 2 Corinthians, Paul describes the beginnings of the Christian life in precisely these terms. "The god of this world," that is, Satan, "has blinded the minds of the unbelievers." As a result, unbelievers are kept "from seeing the light of the gospel of the glory of Christ, who is the image of God" (2 Cor. 4:4).

How does the true and living God overcome the blinding work of the "god of this world"? God "has shone in our hearts to give the light of the knowledge of the glory of God in the face of Jesus Christ" (2 Cor. 4:6). This illumining work dispels the Satanic blindness that once captivated these people. Paul describes this work as nothing less than a work of new creation: "For God, who said, 'Let light shine out of darkness,' has shone in our hearts to give the light of the knowledge of the glory of God in the face of Jesus Christ" (2 Cor. 4:6). Paul is quoting the creation account from Genesis 1:3. The work that Paul is describing in the life of the believer, therefore, is a work of *new* creation. It is a work of sovereign omnipotence. God is active; the creature is acted upon. The effect of this work, Paul stresses, is that human beings are able to perceive "the light of the gospel of the glory of Christ" (2 Cor. 4:4). They not only now intellectually apprehend the message, they also now relish that gospel and incline themselves to it. Specifically, they relish the Christ of that gospel and incline themselves to Him.

But Jesus' work of opening the eyes of human beings when the gospel is preached has another effect. People who have had their eyes opened turn "from the power of Satan to God" (Acts 26:18). To be sure, they are rescued from a state of spiritual blindness. More, however, is in view. Paul elaborates upon this reality in his epistle to the Colossians: "[The Father] has qualified you to share in the inheritance of the saints in light. He has delivered us from the domain of darkness and transferred us to the kingdom of his beloved Son, in whom we have redemption, the forgiveness of sins" (Col. 1:12–14). Paul characterizes the beginnings of the Christian life in terms of a transfer from "darkness" to "light." Formerly, we were under the "domain of darkness." The Father has "transferred us to the kingdom of his beloved Son." In this kingdom dwell "the saints in light," all of whom are heirs.[4] This transfer is from one realm or kingdom (darkness) to another antithetical realm or kingdom (light). Believers are those who have been transferred from one mode of existence and brought into an entirely new mode of existence.

What characterizes the lives of those who have been sovereignly transferred into the kingdom of Christ? They are saints. That is, they are set apart from the world and for God. They are consecrated to Him and called to order the whole of their lives accordingly. They are heirs. They have "redemption," which Paul describes here in terms of "the forgiveness of sins," that is, the remission of "all [their] trespasses" (Col. 1:12, 14; 2:13). It is precisely these notes that Paul sounds in Acts 26:18. The work of Christ in the lives of sinners is such that they "receive forgiveness of sins and a place among those who are sanctified by faith in [Jesus]."[5]

We may summarize the saving work that Jesus Christ does in the lives of men and women who hear the gospel that Paul was commissioned to preach in these terms: People are brought from Satanic darkness to divine light. They are rescued from Satan's dominion into the kingdom of Christ. They are forgiven, sanctified, and made heirs. They are enabled to believe in Jesus Christ as the risen Savior and Lord. Not only did Paul's hearers experience these realities, but Paul himself experienced these realities at his conversion on the Damascus Road. It was Christ's purpose that the one who would bring the gospel to the nations would have firsthand experience of the saving power of that gospel in his own life.

## Lessons for Today

What lessons does the account of Paul's call and conversion afford the church today? We may point to at least three. First, Paul's call and conversion show that salvation is by grace alone. Paul was a man possessed of many natural

---

4   Compare Paul's words later in Acts 26:18: "and a place among those who are sanctified by faith in me." Some commentators have argued that the Greek word underlying the translation "place" is best rendered "inheritance."

5   Not only "sanctified" but also "forgiveness of sins" and "a place" are qualified as happening "by faith in me" (Acts 26:18). The whole of the Christian life is defined and qualified by faith in Jesus Christ (see Gal. 2:20). It is through faith in Christ that believers have each of the benefits described in Acts 26:18.

abilities and accomplishments. But they were all placed in the service of sin. Paul thought he was rendering service to God when he persecuted the church, and he sincerely believed that he was faithful to God's covenant (see Phil. 3:6). But in reality, he was serving the world, the flesh, and the devil (see Eph. 2:1–3). The one word that Paul would use at the end of his life to describe himself before the Damascus Road is "sinner" (1 Tim. 1:15).

On the Damascus Road and immediately afterward, Paul was made the subject of a work of new creation. God brought him from one domain (Satan's) to another (the kingdom of Christ). In so doing, God was setting the entirety of Paul's life upon a brand-new foundation. Paul did not cooperate with God or take steps toward God to bring these realities into being. They were exclusively the work of the sovereign God. Neither did God do these things to Paul because He found moral worth in Paul or the promise of virtue or usefulness in the service of His kingdom. As Paul would later testify to the Corinthians, "by the grace of God I am what I am" (1 Cor. 15:10). Paul was acted upon, and God alone was the One who saved him, and that by an exercise of sovereign, divine power and grace. This experience reflects two of the core principles of Paul's theology: the sheer helplessness and unworthiness of the human sinner and the invincible might of God's mercy in Christ.

Second, we learn that those whom God saves, He puts into service. Paul was both called and commissioned. That is to say, he was called savingly from darkness to light and, at the same time, he was commissioned to service in Christ's name. Paul's commission consisted of bearing witness to the risen Christ before Jews and Gentiles. Luke's account shows that Paul complied with that commission. In Paul's own words to King Agrippa, "I was not disobedient to the heavenly vision, but declared first to those in Damascus, then in Jerusalem and throughout all the region of Judea, and also to the Gentiles, that they should repent and turn to God, performing deeds in keeping with their repentance" (Acts 26:19–20). Paul's summons to others to "repent and turn to God" was founded upon Paul's testimony to Jesus. In Damascus, therefore, "immediately [Paul] proclaimed Jesus in the synagogues saying, 'He is the Son of God'" (Acts 9:20), "proving that Jesus was the Christ" (Acts 9:22).

To be sure, Paul's Apostolic commission was a unique one. Subsequent generations of Christians cannot bear the unique and authoritative witness to the risen Christ that the Apostle Paul did. Nor is every Christian called to preach the gospel, as Paul was and some Christians are. But every Christian is called to serve Christ—in his family, school, place of business, and the church. A sizable portion of Paul's letters is dedicated to helping believers understand Christ's claims upon them in these spheres.

Third, we learn that those whom God saves, He puts into His family. The first recorded words that the Apostle Paul heard from the lips of a fellow Christian were those of Ananias: "Brother Saul" (Acts 9:17; 22:13). When one becomes a Christian, he is immediately brought into a spiritual family and has countless brothers and sisters in Christ. For this reason, Paul immediately began to associate with his new family. As soon as he was baptized and had regained his strength, he was "with the disciples" (Acts 9:19). Soon thereafter in Jerusalem, "he attempted to join the disciples" (Acts 9:26). Even though "they were all afraid of him, for they did not believe that he was a disciple," Paul did not give up on the church of Jerusalem (Acts 9:26). Thanks to Barnabas' help, Paul was able to go "in and out among them at Jerusalem" (Acts 9:28). The Christian life, Paul shows us, is not a solitary one. To be sure, God saves individuals, but He does not call His children to live individualistically. He calls them to live in a special community—the church—that He has formed and set apart for Himself. When we read Paul's letters, we cannot but be impressed with this reality. Paul's letters are filled with the so-called "one another" commands. Large tracts of Paul's letters would be unintelligible and inapplicable apart from the reality of believers' living in recognized relationship with other local Christians. The church, Paul knew, is no mere voluntary organization or association of like-minded individuals. It is a spiritual family created by God the Father in His Son, Jesus Christ, through the power of the Spirit of the Son. Paul's teaching in his Epistles helps God's people understand what it means to be part of God's family and to live faithfully as members of God's family.

# Chapter 3

---

# PAUL'S GOSPEL
# AND THE TWO AGES

When Paul was called and converted on the Damascus Road, he experienced the grace of Christ, whom he would devote the remainder of his life to proclaiming. Paul told the Galatians that he received from Jesus Christ both a gospel to preach (Gal. 1:11–12) and a commission to preach Christ (Gal. 1:16). *Christ* and the *gospel*, of course, were not two different and non-intersecting messages committed to Paul. Paul had a single message. He was called to preach the good news that is about Jesus Christ, the good news that finds its center and circumference in the person and work of Jesus Christ.

Given the importance of the gospel to Paul's life and theology, discerning precisely what Paul understands the gospel to be is a worthwhile endeavor. Thankfully, Paul has given us ample materials to guide our reflection. With respect to the question of Paul's conception of the gospel, we may point to a long answer and a short answer in Paul's writings.

The long answer is Paul's epistle to the Romans. In Romans 1:16–17, Paul indicates that the thesis or main point of the letter concerns the gospel that Paul preaches. Paul then goes on to devote nearly sixteen chapters to unpacking this message of good news to the church at Rome.

We may identify at least two reasons for the gospel focus of Paul's letter to the Romans. First, Paul writes from Corinth (see Rom. 16:1–2, 23) at an important juncture in his ministry. He is preparing to go to Jerusalem to present an offering gathered from Paul's Gentile churches to the churches in Jerusalem (see Rom. 15:22–33). This offering will be a public, palpable, and powerful expression of the church's unity across Jewish and Gentile lines. It is the gospel that Paul unfolds in Romans that provides the foundation for and motive of this unity (Rom. 1:16–17). It seems, as well, that the Roman believers stood to benefit directly from hearing this message once again (Rom. 1:15). There are more than a few hints of division in the church at Rome itself (see Rom. 14:1–15:13). The Roman Christians would need to rehearse the gospel and its implications in order to give a more adequate visual expression of their unity in Christ.

Second, Paul surveys his Apostolic labors in the eastern Mediterranean basin and judges that those labors have come to a certain degree of completion (see Rom. 15:19, 23). He is now ready to preach "not where Christ has already been named, lest I build on someone else's foundation" (Rom. 15:20). Paul intends, then, to travel to Spain after he visits Jerusalem (Rom. 15:24). He plans, however, to stop in Rome before he goes to Spain. Paul desires to help the Roman Christians by preaching the gospel to them (Rom. 1:15). He also hopes to be "helped" by the church in Rome (Rom. 15:24), likely a reference to the anticipated financial and prayer support of this church in advance of his Spanish mission. To that end, Paul offers to the church, in the form of this letter, a summary of the gospel that he preaches. The more that the church is aware of the message that Paul preaches, the more inclined they will be to lend their assistance to his ministry.

We will look more carefully at this long answer in later chapters. Thankfully, Paul has also provided us a short answer in 1 Corinthians 15:1–5:

Now I would remind you, brothers, of the gospel I preached to you, which you received, in which you stand, and by which you are being saved, if you hold fast to the word I preached to you—unless you believed in vain. For I delivered to you as of first importance what I also received: that Christ died for our sins in accordance with the Scriptures, that he was buried, that he was raised on the third day in accordance with the Scriptures, and that he appeared to Cephas, then to the twelve.

What does Paul say about his gospel in these verses? We may note at least three things. First, at the heart of the good news that Paul proclaimed are two historical works of Christ—His death and resurrection: "Christ died for our sins" and "he was raised on the third day." These two works are well attested or proven historical facts: Jesus' burial confirms His death; Jesus' postresurrection appearances confirm His resurrection.[1] Furthermore, both Jesus' death and resurrection are said to be "in accordance with the Scriptures" (1 Cor. 15:3–4). That is to say, Jesus' death and resurrection were of such central importance and concern that God had long ago spoken of them in the Old Testament to His people. God had sent His servants the prophets to declare these future historical events as the substance of Israel's hope. Israel's hoped-for Messiah, Paul affirms, had in fact come to earth and accomplished in history all that was needed for His people's salvation.

Second, the gospel assumes that human beings are sinners: "Christ died for our sins."[2] All human beings, apart from the intervention of saving grace, are held captive to sin and spiritually dead in sin (see Eph. 2:1–3). There is, of course, one shining exception to this sad pattern—the man Christ Jesus. Christ was a true man, but Christ did not commit sin or possess a sinful nature.[3] In these respects, then, He was qualified to be our Redeemer.

The gospel does not merely inform human beings of their native depravity; it is also a message of salvation to sinners: "[the gospel] by which you are being saved" (1 Cor. 15:2). The gospel is, as Paul puts it elsewhere, the "gospel of your salvation" (Eph. 1:13). The reason that Paul declares the

---

1  Christ's burial does not have coordinate significance with His death and resurrection. It serves, rather, as evidence or proof of Jesus' death. In this respect, it is analogous to the postresurrection appearances of Jesus to people described in 1 Corinthians 15:5–8. These appearances offered proof that Jesus had in fact been raised from the dead.

2  That Paul preached this message to universal audiences confirms his belief in the universal sinfulness of humanity.

3  Paul gives expression to Christ's impeccability at Philippians 2:7 and Romans 8:3. In Philippians 2:7, Paul says that Jesus was "born in the likeness of men." In Romans 8:3, Paul says that the Father "sen[t] his own Son in the likeness of sinful flesh and for sin." The phrase "in the likeness of" serves in both passages to distance Jesus from humanity in one respect and one respect only—sinfulness. The importance of Christ's sinlessness is evident in both passages by the thought that immediately follows these expressions. It was the sinless Christ who offered Himself for the sins of sinners. He had to be a pure, spotless, and righteous sacrifice in order to be an acceptable sacrifice for our sins.

death and resurrection of Christ to sinners is so that sinners may be saved by Christ from their sin.

Third, while the gospel saves, it is not automatically saving. Paul insists that the gospel must be "preached," and that it must also be "received" (1 Cor. 15:1). God has appointed a work both for the messenger and the audience. What does it mean to "receive" the gospel? It means, in brief, to believe the gospel (1 Cor. 15:2, "unless you *believed* in vain"; v. 11, "whether then it was I or they, so we preach and so you *believed*"; emphasis added). The character of this faith is that it grasps Jesus Christ, offered in the gospel, and continues to hold on. Believers "stand" in the gospel and "hold fast to the word . . . preached" (v. 2). Faith, then, is not a momentary experience. There is, to be sure, an initial act of faith in receiving the Lord Jesus Christ. But this faith continues in its commitment to Christ and to the gospel that brings Christ near to the believer.

## Gospel Theology

Paul's theology, then, is fairly described as a "gospel theology," the "center" of which is "the death and resurrection of Christ."[4] Much of our work in the remainder of this book will consist of exploring what the precise contents of Paul's gospel are. We will do so along the lines of sin and salvation, following the logical sequence that Paul himself follows in his presentations of his "gospel theology."

Before we turn to these specific details, we need to step back and reflect upon the fundamentally *historical* character of the gospel. For Paul, as for the other biblical writers, the gospel is not a compilation of timeless truths abstracted from history. Neither is it a verbal expression of the religious experiences of a particular group of people. It is the declaration of historical facts—specifically, what God in Christ has accomplished in history.

To appreciate this indispensable dimension of Paul's gospel, we need to ask how Paul, in concert with the other New Testament writers, understood history, particularly in light of the life and ministry of Jesus Christ. For Paul, history is linear and progressive, and it moves toward a set goal. History has as its starting point the creation, when God spoke the world and everything in it into existence (1 Cor. 8:6; Col. 1:16). History reaches

---

4 Richard B. Gaffin Jr., *By Faith, Not by Sight*, 2nd ed. (Phillipsburg, N.J.: P&R, 2013), 27.

its consummation or conclusion when Christ returns in glory to judge the world (1 Thess. 4:13–5:11). At that time, Paul tells us, the creation "will be set free from its bondage to corruption and obtain the freedom of the glory of the children of God" (Rom. 8:21), and "all things" will be "subjected" to God, who will be "all in all" (1 Cor. 15:28).

The center, or midpoint, of history, according to the New Testament writers, is the incarnation, death, and exaltation of Jesus Christ. But Jesus Christ does more than simply occupy the center of history. Writing to the Galatians, Paul identifies the moment when "God sent forth his Son, born of woman, born under the law" as "the fullness of time" (Gal. 4:4). Writing to the Ephesians, Paul speaks of the ministry of Christ broadly in terms of "the fullness of time" (Eph. 1:10). Paul is saying that Christ's ministry has brought history to its intended fulfillment and conclusion.[5] The finished work of Christ, therefore, is the climax of the history of humanity and affords that history its fundamental meaning. It is in Christ that "all things . . . things in heaven and things on earth" find their point of integration (Eph. 1:10).[6]

Christians have given expression to this reality by denominating history as "BC" or "AD." That is to say, what was thought to be the year in which Christ was born (AD 1) becomes a bright line of chronological division. Events and people before the birth of Christ fall in the years "BC" (Before Christ). Events and people after the birth of Christ fall in the years "AD" (Latin *Anno Domini*—in the year of our Lord).

The New Testament writers employ a different convention to express the momentous implications of the incarnation and public ministry of Christ for human history. That convention is that of the two ages, that is, "this age" and "the age to come." Although this terminology does not appear to have been used, as such, by the Old Testament writers, it faithfully expresses realities addressed within the Old Testament.

The Old Testament authors understood the world in which we live to be God's world—created and sustained by the living and true God. This world, however, has fallen under God's curse because of Adam's sin. As a

---

5  Herman Ridderbos, *Paul: An Outline of His Theology*, trans. J.R. DeWitt (Grand Rapids, Mich.: Eerdmans, 1975), 44–45.

6  However imperfectly realized this reality is now, Paul's point is that the cosmos is in the present time finding its reintegration in the exalted and enthroned Christ.

result, our world is now marred by sin and death. There is no hope to be found for the world within the world itself. The world's hope, rather, is found in the saving mercies of Yahweh, the God of Israel. The prophets point God's people to a future in which God would come to earth in order to judge the world and to save His people (Jew and Gentile). His appearing would lift the curse from the creation and usher in the new heavens and new earth. This saving work of God, the prophets tell us, is tied to the appearance of God's Servant, His Messiah.

Jewish authors who wrote after the period of the Old Testament used the "two age" terminology to express this state of affairs.[7] "This age" denotes the world as we presently experience it—created, fallen, under God's curse, characterized by sin and death. "The age to come" denotes the new order that God will usher into history when He appears in salvation and judgment. It describes the world with the effects of the fall removed and the world brought to its intended consummation as a place where righteousness dwells and reigns. Whereas the present age is marked by curse, death, and shame, the age to come is marked by blessing, life, and glory.

The New Testament writers understood the historical work of the incarnate Christ to be the decisive point of transition between the two ages. God had come to earth in the person of Jesus Christ. Jesus Christ is the Son of God become flesh; David's Son and David's Lord; fully divine and fully human. This incarnate Son was sent by the Father, as God's Servant, the promised Messiah. In His obedience, death, and exaltation, Jesus undertook all that His people need to be brought from death to life, from curse to blessing. Not only will they experience this new life and blessing to the full, but they will do so in a world freed from sin and death and renewed in righteousness.

The New Testament's use of the phrases "this age" and "the age to come" helps us understand the significance of Christ and His ministry. In the teaching of Jesus, we see Jesus employing both phrases at Matthew 12:32: "Whoever speaks against the Holy Spirit will not be forgiven, either in this age or in the age to come" (see also Eph. 1:21).[8] In Luke 20:34–35, Jesus

---

7 For examples, see Geerhardus Vos, *The Pauline Eschatology* (1930; repr., Phillipsburg, N.J.: P&R, 1994), 22–24.

8 In context, the Holy Spirit spoken against is the Holy Spirit who is active in the public ministry of Jesus on earth.

says that "the sons of this age marry and are given in marriage," but those who belong to "that age" are they who "attain" the "resurrection from the dead," and "neither marry nor are given in marriage." The "age to come," Jesus tells us, is characterized by the life of the resurrection and, with respect to the institution of marriage, differs from "this age."

Jesus' Apostle Paul then gives us a fuller and more detailed account of these realities. For Paul, three things characterize "this age" or the "world."[9] First, this age is "evil"—he calls it "the present evil age" (Gal. 1:4). It stands in decided, uncompromised, and stark moral opposition to and rebellion against God. It is characterized by "trespasses and sins" (Eph. 2:1).

Second, the participation of unbelievers in this age is comprehensive. That is to say, there is no aspect of their persons that is not characterized and determined by whatever characterizes this age. Their thinking, choosing, and behavior are all affected. This age, Paul argues, has a way of thinking. That is why he urges believers, "Do not be conformed to this world [lit. "age"], but be transformed by the renewal of your mind" (Rom. 12:2; see 1 Cor. 1:21–22). There are inclinations and affections that characterize attachment to this age. Paul describes the apostate Demas as "in love with this present world" (2 Tim. 4:10). There are also patterns of behavior and life that characterize this age. For this reason, Paul can characterize believers' formerly belonging to this age in terms of "the trespasses and sins in which you once walked, following the course of this world" (Eph. 2:1–2).

Third, Paul understands this present age as a corporate reality. It involves individuals, but it is bigger than any one individual. Thus, Paul can identify Satan as "the god of this world" (2 Cor. 4:4) and speak of the world as having a "wisdom" all its own, one that is opposed to God and that God has demonstrated at the cross to be foolish (see 1 Cor. 1:18–2:16). There is a supra-individual solidarity to the sinful thinking, choosing, and behaving of fallen men and women.

In contrast to "this age" is the "age to come." Although Paul only uses a form of the latter expression one time (Eph. 1:21; yet see 2:7; 1 Cor. 10:11), it captures something that is all-important for Paul—the new order that

---

9   That "this age" and the "world" are interchangeable expressions for Paul is evident from his argument in the opening chapters of 1 Corinthians, where Paul can speak of "the wisdom of the world" (1:20), and then the "wisdom of this age" (2:6), and then "the wisdom of this world" (3:19). Each of these phrases refers to the same reality.

Christ has ushered into history by His death and resurrection. It is into this new order that Christ brings each of His people. We have seen Paul describe this order as a *kingdom*: "He has delivered us from the domain of darkness and transferred us to the kingdom of his beloved Son" (Col. 1:13). He elsewhere describes it as *new creation*: "Therefore, if anyone is in Christ— new creation!" (2 Cor. 5:17, author's translation).[10] It is this reality of new creation that corresponds to the phrase "the age to come." Ordinarily, Paul describes this reality when he speaks of believers as savingly united to Christ (i.e., "in Christ," "with Christ"). In union with Jesus Christ, and by the ministry of the Holy Spirit who binds us to Christ, we share in all that Christ has won for us in His obedience, death, and exaltation.

Believers, then, in union with Christ, have been brought decisively into the age to come. This means that we have been decisively delivered from *this age*. Christ "gave himself for our sins to deliver us from the present evil age" (Gal. 1:4). We are accordingly said to have been delivered from *this world*. Paul speaks of the "cross of our Lord Jesus Christ" as that "by which the world has been crucified to me, and I to the world" (Gal. 6:14). We therefore have a brand-new relationship with *sin*. We have "died to sin" (Rom. 6:2) and therefore are no longer under its "dominion" (Rom. 6:14). We are, rather, "alive to God in Christ Jesus" (Rom. 6:11). This new life is ours because, united with Jesus Christ, God has already "made us alive together with Christ" and "raised us up with him" (Eph. 2:5–6).

And yet, believers have yet to experience fully the age to come. Unless Jesus returns beforehand, believers will die. Our bodies will most certainly be raised, but we do not yet possess our resurrection bodies. Our bodies now are mortal and perishable. We await the day when our bodies will be immortal and imperishable (see 1 Cor. 15:1–58). We have already begun to experience the glory of God (2 Cor. 3:17–18), but our full experience of that glory remains a "hope" for us (Rom. 5:2). Until we experience consummate glory with Christ, we must be prepared to suffer with Christ (Rom. 8:17).

---

10 The ESV renders this verse, "Therefore, if anyone is in Christ, he is a new creation." There are no words in the Greek corresponding to the English "he is a." The ESV's translation is not mistaken but it fails to capture the fullness of what Paul is saying. To be united with Christ is to be translated or ushered into an entirely new order. The difference between the believer's previous existence outside of Christ and his current existence in Christ is so radical that Paul employs the word "creation" to capture it.

What's more, believers continue to live in this age. As Paul explains to Titus, the grace of God in Christ "train[s] us to renounce ungodliness and worldly passions, and to live self-controlled, upright, and godly lives in the present age" (Titus 2:12). We have been rescued *from* the present age, we are no longer *of* the present age, but we continue to live *in* the present age.

How may we explain this puzzling state of affairs? Believers live in what has been called the "overlap of the ages." That is to say, we have already begun to experience the age to come, but we have not yet experienced it fully or completely. Similarly, we have been decisively delivered from this present age, but we are called to live our Christian lives within this present age or world.

One place in Paul's letters that best captures and calibrates this dynamic is Romans 8. In this grand chapter, Paul is delineating the ministry of the Spirit in the lives of believers. In verses 5–11, he speaks of two modes of existence—"flesh" and "Spirit." These two modes of existence correspond to the two ages we have been surveying in this chapter.[11] For Paul, human beings are not neutral. They do not stand in equilibrium between "flesh" and "Spirit." Each person is determined in the whole of his being either by "flesh" or by "Spirit." Believers, by definition, "walk not according to the flesh but according to the Spirit" (v. 4). We "live according to the Spirit" and "set [our] minds on the things of the Spirit" (v. 5). Put simply, we "are not in the flesh but in the Spirit" (v. 9). One knows that he is "in the Spirit" if "the Spirit of God dwells in [him]" (v. 9). The Spirit indwells believers and directs and determines the whole course of their thinking, choosing, and living.

But in this very passage, Paul gives warnings to those who profess to be "in the Spirit." We are not to "walk . . . according to the flesh," "live according to the flesh," or "set [our] minds on the things of the flesh" (Rom. 8:4–5). Those who do so are "in the flesh," and such people "cannot please God" (v. 8). Even those who are "in the Spirit" and not "in the flesh" may find that the old, fleshly patterns of thinking and living are never terribly

---

11 In contrasting "flesh" with "Spirit," Paul is not contrasting the passions with reason, or the body with the soul. For Paul, the "works of the flesh" include not only the actions of the body but also the desires and thoughts of the soul (see Gal. 5:19–21). The distinction in Romans 8, rather, touches on two ways of living—one that which is pleasing to and conforms to the mind of the Holy Spirit, and one that which stands in opposition to the Holy Spirit. Or, in terms of the categories that Paul has introduced in Romans 5:12–21, "flesh" describes life "in Adam"; "Spirit" describes life "in Christ." "Flesh" and "Spirit" are two alternate modes of existence that describe the orientation, mind-set, and lifestyle of the whole person.

distant. For this reason, Paul calls us "by the Spirit" to "put to death the deeds of the body," and so to "live" (v. 13).

The Christian, then, remains in a place of threat and danger so long as he is in this world. The temptations afforded by the world, the flesh, and the devil can never be discounted or underestimated. Even so, the true believer is never in bondage to the world, the flesh, and the devil. On the contrary, he is freed from their dominion and lives under the lordship of Jesus Christ. In Christ, believers have all the resources they need to live in ways that are pleasing to their Savior and Lord. Not least of these resources is the supply of the Spirit who indwells them. This reality does not render the believer passive or indifferent to the threats that lie at hand. This reality, rather, calls and stirs the believer to be vigilant and active in saying no to sin and in living to the glory of Christ.

## Lessons for Today

Understanding these dynamics is crucial to a well-formed understanding of the gospel that Paul preached, and Paul's explanations help us live the Christian life well. First, Paul moves us toward a clearer understanding of our sin. Formerly we were given over to sin. Although we have been decisively delivered from sin's dominion, there are forces without and within (the world, the flesh, and the devil) that tempt and threaten us to sin. We are by no means helpless, but we cannot afford to be heedless. Understanding who we once were as sinners and our new relationship with sin as believers is crucial to our effectively engaging the enemy—sin.

Second, Paul moves us toward a clearer understanding of the grace of Christ. Grace is not an "add on" to the resources we are able to muster from within ourselves. On the contrary, once savingly united to Christ, Christians possess all the resources they need to live for Christ, resources that are provided by the grace of Christ alone (1 Cor. 4:7). As we live in the tension and conflict of life between the times, that is, between the "already" and the "not yet," we ought to strive and strain in confidence. The world, the flesh, and the devil are no match for Christ and the Spirit. To understand what these resources are and how we come to share in them, we need to give further attention to Paul's gospel.

Chapter 4

# PAUL'S GOSPEL—SIN (I)

In 1973, the psychiatrist Karl Menninger published a book titled *Whatever Became of Sin?* If that question was a relevant one for American culture more than forty years ago, it is at least as relevant today. Sadly, it is a question that may be fairly put to many quarters of the American church. Sin seems to have lost its currency in both culture and church.

It may seem strange to launch a discussion of Paul's gospel with the topic of sin. But, as we shall see, sin is not a strange starting point at all. Sin is precisely where Paul begins his own discussions of the gospel. The gospel is a message of salvation, and our sin is one of the things from which we are saved. We may go so far as to say that Paul's gospel is meaningless without a clear understanding of the sin that occasions the need for that gospel.

This fact explains the approach that Paul takes in Romans. He announces his "gospel thesis" at Romans 1:16–17—the gospel is the "power of God for salvation to everyone who believes, to the Jew first and also to the Greek." In the gospel, "the righteousness of God is revealed from faith for faith." But it will not be until Romans 3:21 that Paul begins to discuss what this "righteousness of God" is. From Romans 1:18–3:20, Paul treats us to an extended, two-and-a-half-chapter discussion of human sin.

Why does Paul spend so much time on sin, and why does he make that discussion a matter of first priority in Romans? The reason is that, before one can rightly understand, value, and desire the "righteousness of God," he must know that he both lacks and needs this righteousness. To that end, Paul sets out to prove the universal unrighteousness of humanity.

Paul unfolds that proof in three parts. First, he dwells on the unrighteousness of humanity with particular attention to the Gentile (Rom. 1:18–31). Second, he dwells on the unrighteousness of humanity with particular attention to the Jew (Rom. 2:1–3:8). Third, he brings his argument to a powerful summary and conclusion (Rom. 3:9–20). In this chapter, we will survey each of these three sections of Paul's brief against depraved humanity.

## The Woeful Human Condition

In a way similar to other biblical writers, Paul divides humanity into two groups. There are Jews, the covenant people of God, and there are Gentiles, or everyone else (the word *Gentile* is derived from a Latin word meaning "nation" or "people"). Paul says in Romans 1:16 that the gospel is "to the Jew first and also to the Greek." It is precisely along these lines that Paul establishes the universal need for this gospel. While speaking about all humanity, he gives particular attention in this opening section to the Gentiles.

Paul's opening line in Romans 1:18 echoes what he has said in verse 17. Romans 1:17 speaks of the "righteousness of God" that the gospel brings to human beings. In Romans 1:18, however, Paul's concern is the "wrath of God" that proceeds "from heaven against all ungodliness and unrighteousness of men." The "wrath of God" is not uncontrolled rage, the way we sometimes experience wrath in ourselves and from others. It is God's holy and just hatred of sin ("all ungodliness and unrighteousness of men"). God hates sin and can never be reconciled to it. Neither can He ignore it. What Paul describes in this verse is the way in which God's hatred of sin comes to expression in the world around us.

What we see of God's wrath in the world today is only a hint of what is to come in full on the day of judgment. Paul calls that day a "day of wrath when God's righteous judgment will be revealed" (Rom. 2:5). The wrath of God in history now is a signpost or pointer to the full outpouring of the divine wrath that will come at the end of history.

Paul's declaration raises an important question: How can God judge all human beings? Multitudes have never seen a Bible, heard the Christian gospel, or had any meaningful contact with Christian people. On what basis can God justly judge them?

Paul provides a thorough answer to that question in this passage. All human beings are accountable to God because all human beings know God (Rom. 1:21). How do they know Him? They know Him "in the things that have been made" (v. 20). What do they know of God? They know "his invisible attributes, namely, his eternal power and divine nature" (v. 20). Do they really understand this knowledge? Yes, these truths are "clearly perceived" (v. 20); "what can be known about God is plain to them, because God has shown it to them" (v. 19). Does this reality pertain to all ages and places of the world? Yes, these attributes of God are known "ever since the creation of the world, in the things that have been made" (v. 20).

All human beings, then, are "without excuse" (Rom. 1:20). They rebel against the God they know from creation: "For although they knew God, they did not honor him as God or give thanks to him, but they became futile in their thinking, and their foolish hearts were darkened" (v. 21). There is, Paul notes, a lamentable exchange: "[They] exchanged the glory of the immortal God for images resembling mortal man and birds and animals and creeping things" (v. 23); "they exchanged the truth about God for a lie and worshiped and served the creature rather than the Creator, who is blessed forever! Amen" (v. 25). In sum, human beings turn from the worship of God to the worship of the creature; from the truth to a lie; from the glory of God to the shame of idols.

Paul does not regard the world's religions as so many attempts on the part of people to get closer to God. The opposite is the case: human-crafted religion, in all its varied expressions, is sinful humanity's attempt to get away from God. It is an expression of hatred and rejection of God. Apart from the true religion that God alone has revealed, all religion is man-made and built on a lie. It is the substitution of dead idols for the living God (see 1 Thess. 1:9).

Human beings' rebellion against God spills over into our relationships with one another. That is to say, our relationship with God determines our relationships with human beings. Three times, Paul says that God "gives up" idolatrous human beings to the sins that they want (Rom. 1:24–32). This judicial abandonment has devastating effects on human interrelations. In Romans 1:24, Paul says that God has given up people "in the lusts of their hearts to impurity, to the dishonoring of their bodies among themselves." In verses 26–27, Paul says that God "gave [people] up to dishonorable passions . . . men . . . receiving in themselves the due penalty for their error."

In verse 28, Paul says that "God gave [people] up to a debased mind to do what ought not to be done," with numerous devastating consequences on the plane of human existence (see vv. 29–32).

In this discussion of the divine "giving over," Paul highlights a particular sin, namely, same-sex relations (Rom. 1:26–27). In accenting this sin in the way that he does, Paul is not saying that this is an unforgivable sin. In 1 Corinthians 6:11, Paul says that the Corinthians, some of whom had practiced this very sin (see 1 Cor. 6:9), were "washed," "sanctified," and "justified." One reason why Paul highlights this sin has to do with the fact that it is "contrary to nature" (Rom. 1:26; see the word "natural" at vv. 26–27). By "nature," Paul does not mean "what we observe going on in the world around us." He means, rather, "in keeping with our natures as human beings made after the image of God." God has made humanity male and female. To commit the sin of same-sex relations is to refuse to live in the way that God has created us to live. Same-sex relations are a sin against the God who made us male and female and who ordained marriage for our good as human beings. As such, it is a vivid instance of the rebellion that Paul is describing in Romans 1.

The sinful creativity of the human heart is seemingly unbounded. In Romans 1:29–32, Paul lists more than twenty vices. We may note three observations about this grim description of the human condition. First, the lead vice in verse 29 is that human beings "were filled with all manner of unrighteousness." The word "unrighteousness" characterizes the depravity of the human condition. It is also precisely what Paul intends to prove in this opening section of Romans. Our dilemma is that, as unrighteous humans, we cannot stand before a righteous God. We are in need of a righteousness that we do not have and cannot produce.

Second, most of the sins in these few verses are committed against our fellow human beings. One exception is found in Romans 1:30, where we read that people are "haters of God." The inclusion of this sin is a reminder of Paul's earlier point that our dealings with the people around us are the outworking of our relationship with God. If we hate God, we will not truly love others. Sins against people spring from and are fed by rebellion against God.

Third, the helplessness and hopelessness of the human condition is voiced in the closing verse of this chapter: "Though they know God's righteous decree that those who practice such things deserve to die, they not only do them but give approval to those who practice them" (Rom. 1:32). Sin is deserving of death (Rom. 6:23). People know this divine "decree" and yet continue in the "practice" of sin. To make matters worse, they encourage others to do the same. Such is sin that it drives people not only to destroy themselves but also to hasten the destruction of others.

## The Place of the Jews

Paul's assessment of humanity, and particularly Gentile humanity, is a bleak one. One might ask whether the Jews are at all an exception to this pattern. After all, they are God's old covenant people and have been extended privileges and benefits that no other people in the world have enjoyed. Might there be some hope for humanity within this people?

The Apostle answers with a decided no. Although he does not mention the Jews by name until Romans 2:17, it is likely that the Jews are the focus of Paul's argument in Romans 2:1–3:8. What he says about the Jews has application to the church today.

Paul begins with the Jew who "pass[es] judgment on another" (Rom. 2:1). It is not wrong, of course, to render just judgments. The Apostle's concern, however, is that "you, the judge, practice the very same things." Therefore, when such a one passes judgment, he condemns himself (v. 1). Paul is speaking of the tendency of God's covenant people to condemn outsiders even as they themselves refuse to repent of the very sins that they condemn. Such people, he stresses, will not "escape the judgment of God" (v. 3). That they have sinned against God's "kindness and forbearance and patience" will only aggravate their judgment (vv. 4–5).

God is an impartial God (Rom. 2:11). He will condemn "every human being who does evil, the Jew first and also the Greek" (v. 9), even as He will reward "everyone who does good, the Jew first and also the Greek" (v. 10). God's covenant people's proximity to Him will not mitigate or excuse their sins. God is righteous and His judgments are just.

Paul then turns to two examples of ways in which Israel has misused her covenantal privileges—the law (Rom. 2:12–24) and circumcision (vv. 25–29). Every human being, the Apostle insists, knows God and His moral requirements. Gentiles do not possess the Mosaic law (v. 14). They do, however, have "the work of the law . . . written on their hearts," and "their conscience also bears witness" (v. 15).[1] The Jews, however, have more than this. They have the law of God, that is, the law of Moses (Rom. 3:1–2).[2] They are well instructed in that law and even fancy themselves "a guide to the blind, a light to those who are in darkness, an instructor of the foolish, a teacher of children, having in the law the embodiment of knowledge and truth" (Rom. 2:19–20). There are, however, two serious and related problems. The first is that God's people "rely on the law" and "boast in the law" (Rom. 2:17, 23). The second is that, while they understand the law's requirements, they do not do what the law requires of them (Rom. 2:21–24). But righteousness comes not merely by hearing the law, but by perfectly keeping the law also (Rom. 2:13). Many of Paul's Jewish contemporaries were seeking righteousness by law keeping. But they had not found it (see Rom. 9:30–10:4). They were knowledgeable transgressors of God's law. As a result, God was being dishonored and blasphemed (Rom. 2:23–24). Even God's old covenant people stood unrighteous before a righteous and impartial God. They failed to attain by their law keeping the righteousness that God requires.

The second way in which Israel has misused her covenant privileges concerns circumcision (Rom. 2:25–29). Paul is clear: "circumcision indeed is of value"—if one "obey[s] the law" (v. 25). Circumcised individuals who break the law are no different from an uncircumcised person. Suppose an uncircumcised Gentile were to keep God's law perfectly. In that case, God would regard him as a circumcised person, and He would rise up to condemn the transgressor who is physically circumcised (vv. 26–27).

In laying out these hypotheticals, Paul is stressing that the covenant sign and seal of circumcision was never intended to provide sanctuary to violators of God's commandments. An outward ordinance has no power to render a person acceptable before God. Circumcision does not make a person righteous. What counts, Paul says, is the heart. The true member

---

1  By the "work of the law" Paul refers to the moral core of the Mosaic law. The fact that he uses the word "law" in this verse indicates continuity with the law that God gave to Israel through Moses, even as the phrase "work of the law" distinguishes what God has revealed to all people from the fullness of what He has revealed to Israel. That Paul has in mind the moral core of the law is evident from his consistently moral indictment of humanity (including Gentiles) in Romans 1:18–32; see Romans 2:6–11.

2  Typically, for Paul, the word "law" refers to the Mosaic law given to Israel in Exodus 20ff.

of God's people is not identified externally but inwardly—"A Jew is one inwardly, and circumcision is a matter of the heart, by the Spirit, not by the letter" (Rom. 2:29).

Paul concludes his indictment of Israel by stressing that the law (and circumcision) are valuable things in themselves (Rom. 3:1–2). The problem lies not in those good things but in the bad ways that people handle those good things. Our dilemma is that, even within the boundaries of God's covenant, unrighteous people remain subject to the just judgment of the righteous God. It is this fact that explains why Paul shines the uncomfortable spotlight on Israel.[3] Israel is, as it were, humanity's last great hope. She has been given more privileges and helps than any other nation on earth. If any people could attain to righteousness, surely it would be they—the chosen, covenant people, set apart by circumcision, and entrusted with the oracles of God. But they are, in fact, unrighteous. The pinnacle of humanity is unable to find resources from within to stand righteous before God.

## All Humanity under Condemnation

The third and final section of Paul's argument brings his indictment of the human race to a powerful conclusion (Rom. 3:9–20). He begins by stating, "We have already charged that all, both Jews and Greeks, are under sin" (v. 9). Notice that Paul continues to survey and indict humanity along the same two lines: Jew and Gentile. For all their differences, they have in common that they are both "under sin," that is, under the guilt and condemnation of sin and under the dominion and bondage of sin. Neither part of humanity has the wherewithal to escape its predicament.

The following verses (Rom. 3:10–18) offer a scathing and detailed description of this condition. Significantly, Paul cites various passages from across the Old Testament in support of his conclusion. Israel finds herself, with the rest of the nations, indicted and condemned by her own Scriptures. The law, Paul concludes in verse 19, renders those "under the law" both silent and "accountable to God." Even the Gentiles ("the whole world"), who have access to the moral demands of God's law, stand accountable to

---

3 It is sometimes alleged that arguments such as these in Paul's letters evidence the anti-Semitism of the Apostle. Nothing could be further from the truth. Paul the Jew loves the Jewish people, so much so that he "could wish [himself] accursed and cut off from Christ for the sake of [his] brothers, [his] kinsmen according to the flesh" (Rom. 9:3).

God. For this reason, Paul declares, "by works of the law no human being will be justified in his sight, since through the law comes knowledge of sin" (v. 20). No person, Jew or Gentile, can do anything required by the law to render himself righteous before God. To the sinner, rather, the law functions to make him aware of his sin—his transgressions and failings.[4] The law offers no resources and has no power to help the sinner escape his dilemma. If anything, Paul reasons elsewhere, the law only serves as the occasion of accentuating the sinner's dilemma (see Rom. 5:20; 7:7–12).

## Lessons for Today

Such is Paul's grim but necessary bad news that people need to accept before they will be prepared to accept the good news that is the gospel. What lessons does Paul's teaching about sin have for us today? We may point to at least two.

First, the great problem that humanity faces is human sin. Sin is transgressing or failing to meet the righteous standards that God has made known to all human beings. All people know those standards through their consciences. Some have a fuller and clearer statement of those standards as expressed in God's written law. Because these righteous standards reflect the righteous character of God, sin is objectively defined. It is not left to human beings to legislate right and wrong. Right and wrong are established from the eternal and unchanging character of God. Further, all sin is personal. That is to say, sin is an offense not against an impersonal and abstract standard or rule but against a personal God.

One sober truth that Paul teaches here about sin is that God, in judgment, gives sinners over to the sins that they love (Rom. 1:23–28). Very often, people claim to find freedom and fulfillment in indulging themselves in a sinful lifestyle. In reality, being given over to sin is an expression of

---

4 Some recent interpreters have argued that "works of the law" refers to the law's function in identifying an individual as a member of God's covenant people. In other words, these "works of the law" are said to be badges or markers of this identity. To be "justified," it is further argued, has primarily to do with God's declaring someone a member of His people. One significant problem with this line of interpretation is that Paul's concern throughout these opening chapters of Romans is overwhelmingly moral—human beings universally violate God's standards of righteousness. As such, people are unrighteous and justly subject to God's righteous verdict. The "works" in view involve things that they do (or do not do) in keeping with God's law. Paul's main concern in this portion of the letter is simply not with questions of identity and belonging.

God's displeasure. Those who pursue with abandon the sin they love are only preparing for themselves severer judgment on the day of wrath (see Rom. 2:4–5). One of the first lessons that the gospel teaches us is how to think of sin properly—from God's point of view.

A second lesson from Paul's teaching on sin is that there is no hope within us to stand righteous before God. The very best of us is unrighteous, fit only for judgment, wrath, and condemnation on the last day. We cannot look to the law—whether as something that we possess or something that we try to obey—in order to be righteous before God. We cannot rely on circumcision (or baptism), church membership, or church attendance to make us righteous before God (see Gal. 5:6). All of these are powerless to change our condition or to deliver us.

Any hope of salvation must lie outside ourselves. The only hope of mercy for sinners is in this offended God Himself. But how can that be? That is the very next—and glorious—lesson of the gospel that Paul preaches. Before we turn to that lesson, however, we must hear more from Paul about the bad news of our sin.

# Chapter 5

---

# PAUL'S GOSPEL—
# SIN (II)

For Paul, human sinfulness is the great presupposition of the Christian gospel. Apart from our comprehension of sin, the gospel will make little sense to us. For this reason, when Paul announces his gospel in Romans 1:16–17, he does not immediately proceed to explain what that gospel is. Instead, he first explains our need for that gospel in Romans 1:18–3:20.

In these verses, Paul proves that people are universally unrighteous and in need of righteousness. What's more, we have no resources within our fallen humanity to achieve or secure that righteousness. Sin extends to the very core of our being and is directed against the God who reveals Himself in the created order. The wellspring of our sinful thinking, choosing, and behaving is enmity against the God we know. God made us to worship Him and to bring Him glory. Instead, His image bearers have turned their backs on Him and have exchanged the divine glory for the worship and service of the creature.

That is not all that Paul has to say about human sin. In Romans 5:12–21, Paul looks more closely at the roots of human sinfulness. Why is it that sin is an indelible part of our human experience? Why is it that, based on our own experience, we can point to no exceptions to what Paul has been describing about the human condition? Paul's answers to these questions not only seal our helplessness as human sinners but provide the framework within which the gospel announces the help and hope that God offers to sinners.

## The Context for Romans 5:12–20

In Romans 3:21–4:25, which we will explore in the next chapter, Paul explains the gift of righteousness that is offered in the gospel alone. Paul brings the gift itself under the microscope in Romans 3:21–31. In Romans 4:1–25, he shows us how Abraham himself received this gift, through faith alone. Then in Romans 5:1–11, Paul explains the many benefits and blessings that attend this great gift, including "peace with God," "access by faith into this grace in which we stand," "hope of the glory of God," joy in our "sufferings," and the ongoing ministry of the Holy Spirit.

This is the context for Romans 5:12–20. In these verses, Paul wants us to see that these benefits and blessings rest on the surest foundation—the finished work of Christ. To help us see how these benefits and blessings are related to Christ and, therefore, to grasp how they are the secure possession of the believer, Paul undertakes a running comparison and contrast between two representative human beings, Adam and Christ.

We may begin by observing two basic points that Paul makes about Adam and Christ in these verses. First, they are parallel individuals. Their lives and actions have affected human beings in similar ways. Second, even where they are parallel, Christ shines brighter. Paul captures this dynamic of comparison between the two men in the phrase "much more" (Rom. 5:15, 17). Christ's victory far outshines Adam's defeat. In a later chapter, we will give more attention to what Paul says about Christ and His work for believers. In this chapter, we will look at what Paul says about Adam and the implications of his first sin for the human race.

## Adam as Representative

To begin, we need to ask, who is Adam? We may summarize Paul's answer in two ways. First, Adam is the first human being. Paul elsewhere calls him "the first man Adam" (1 Cor. 15:45) or, simply, "the first man" (1 Cor. 15:47). Paul here is summarizing the teaching of Genesis 1–2, the biblical account of the creation of the world, in which we read how God made Adam and Eve, our first parents, of the dust of the ground (see 1 Cor. 15:47, "a man of dust").

It needs to be emphasized that Paul regarded these chapters of Genesis as descriptions of historical events. He did not understand Adam to be a myth or an archetype. He understood Adam to be a fully historical person.

Evidence for this can be seen in that Paul sets Adam in parallel with Christ and Adam's sin in parallel with Christ's obedience. Adam, therefore, can be no less historical a person than Jesus Christ, and Adam's actions in history can be no less historical than Jesus' actions in history. If Christ and His death and resurrection are fully historical ("if Christ has not been raised, your faith is futile and you are still in your sins"; 1 Cor. 15:17), then Adam and his sin are fully historical.

Notice, furthermore, that Paul calls Adam a "type of the one who was to come" (Rom. 5:14). A "type" in Scripture is a correspondence between some lesser historical person or thing and some greater historical person or thing.[1] This relationship of correspondence is one of fulfillment. That is to say, the greater person or thing is the fulfillment of the true meaning or intent of the corresponding lesser person or thing. What is important for our purposes is that biblical types always draw together two *historical* persons or things. This observation confirms that Adam, for Paul, is a true human being—a fully historical and a non-mythological person.

The second way to answer the question of Adam's identity concerns his standing in relation to other human beings. He is a representative figure.[2] To illustrate this, we may think of an analogy in our own day. In many Western countries, citizens elect men and women to represent them in a regional or national legislature. Those representatives act for the citizens in their districts. If the body of representatives votes to raise taxes or to declare war, then that action is the action of all the citizens whom that body represents.

Although we did not elect or choose Adam, God appointed him as the representative of all his posterity.[3] That Adam is our representative means

---

1   I am indebted here to the discussion in J.P. Versteeg, *Adam in the New Testament: Mere Teaching Model or First Historical Man?*, trans. Richard B. Gaffin Jr., 2nd ed. (Phillipsburg, N.J.: P&R, 2012), 9–17.

2   Reformed theologians have often spoken of Adam as "federal" head of the human race. The word *federal* is derived from the Latin word translated into English as "covenant" (*foedus*). It captures Adam's representation of his posterity in the covenant that God made with Adam in the garden. Reformed theology has typically referred to this covenant as the *covenant of works*.

3   Although some have represented this arrangement as unfair, it is, in fact, an action of tremendous generosity to humanity on God's part. A righteous man who had no personal acquaintance with sin, who was living in paradise, who was surrounded by plenty, was given a modest command (to refrain from eating from a single tree) in view of a reward entirely out of proportion to that command. The more we consider these details, the more we see how unjust it is to find fault with this arrangement.

that what Adam did, he did not do merely for himself. He acted on behalf of a body of people whom he represented. He stood for them, so his action became theirs. We see Paul testifying to this reality in his repeated references to Adam as the "one man" (Rom. 5:12, 15, 16, 17, 19). He is set apart from all other human beings descended from him. He is even set apart in this respect from his wife, Eve. Other human beings, by contrast, are termed "all men" (Rom. 5:12, 18) or "the many" (Rom. 5:15, 19). Adam's representation extends to humanity in all times and places.

Yet, there is one human being whom Adam *did not* represent—the man Christ Jesus. Why does Paul refuse to say that Adam represented Christ? It is not because Paul did not believe that Christ was a true human being (1 Tim. 2:5). Christ, after all, is biologically descended from Adam with respect to His humanity (Luke 3:23–38). Paul refuses to say that Adam represented Christ because Christ is the second Man, the last Adam. Jesus does not stand under Adam by nature the way that you and I do. Instead, Jesus stands alongside Adam as the representative of His own people. Jesus, we may say, is *of* or *from* Adam, but He is not *in* Adam.

This state of affairs tells us something important about the relationship between Adam and his posterity in Romans 5:12–21. The relationship in view is representative in nature. God has sovereignly established a bond or union between the representative head, Adam, and the people he represents, that is, the people in Adam, namely, all of his descendants who are merely human. Paul puts it crisply and succinctly in 1 Corinthians 15:22: "In Adam, all die," which we may paraphrase as, "In union with Adam, our representative head, we all die."

Now that we have a clearer grasp of who Adam is, we can look into what it is, according to Paul, that Adam has done. We may survey Paul's teaching in Romans 5:12–21 along three lines. First, Paul's interest is in the first sin of Adam. He is not concerned here with a lifetime or a particular pattern of sinning. Paul speaks rather of "one trespass" (vv. 16, 18) or "the transgression of Adam" (v. 14). The particular sin Paul has in mind is the first sin of Adam in eating the fruit that God forbade him from eating. How do we know? Recall that God threatened Adam with "death" as the consequence of sinning by eating the forbidden fruit ("For in the day that you eat of it you shall surely die"; Gen. 2:17). Paul here understands the "one trespass" of Adam to have unleashed death upon the human race ("If, because of one man's trespass, death reigned through that one man"; Rom. 5:17). He must therefore understand the "one trespass" to be the first sin of Adam.

Second, Paul teaches that Adam's sin was imputed to all human beings whom he represented. The word *impute* means to "reckon," "transfer," or "set to one's account."[4] In this case, Adam's sin is transferred to our account and is reckoned as ours. We are held accountable for that sin because we are in union with Adam our representative head; therefore, his sin is ours. It is this point that Paul emphasizes in Romans 5:12–14. In verse 12, he states the principle, "Death spread to all men because all sinned." He then provides two qualifying statements to help us understand what he means and does not mean by the phrase "all sinned." In verse 14 ("even over those whose sinning was not like the transgression of Adam"), the Apostle excludes our imitation of Adam as the explanation for what Paul means by "all sinned" in verse 12. That is to say, "all sinned" does not mean something like "we have all decided to follow the bad example of Adam in sinning against God." In verse 13 ("For sin indeed was in the world before the law was given, but sin is not counted where there is no law"), Paul excludes our personally or individually transgressing a particular command of God as the explanation for what he means by "all sinned."

Paul means that there is a legal transfer of Adam's sin to his posterity. As a result of this transfer, we are counted liable for Adam's first sin. We bear the consequences of that sin. The framework within which this transfer takes place is our union with our representative, Adam. Because we are in union with Adam, it is just for God to transfer the sin of the representative to those he represents such that we stand legally responsible for that sin.

The third thing Paul does in looking at what Adam has done is to spell out the consequences of the imputation of Adam's sin. In fact, Paul devotes most of his attention in this section to this very thing. In unfolding what it means that Adam's sin has been transferred to us, Paul speaks in a way that confirms that he is thinking judicially or forensically. That is to say, this transfer has taken place in God's courtroom. We may point to three

---

4 "[Impute is] the technical term for that which is expressed by the Greek words in their so-called 'commercial' sense, or what may, more correctly, be called their forensic or 'judicial' sense, 'that is, putting to one's account,' or, in its twofold reference to the credit and debit sides, 'setting to one's credit' or 'laying to one's charge.'" B.B. Warfield, *Studies in Theology* (1932; repr., Grand Rapids, Mich.: Baker, 2000), 301–2.

interrelated forensic consequences that Paul addresses in Romans 5:12–21. First, we are "constituted sinners." We may translate verse 19 thus: "By the one man's disobedience the many were constituted sinners."[5] In the courtroom of God, God counts or reckons those who are in representative union with Adam as "sinners." This reckoning is in view of the one sin of Adam, not of any action that we have done. Paul is not describing here a change that takes place within us. This is not inward transformation. He is describing, rather, a change of status that transpires in God's courtroom. This is a legal change.

The second forensic consequence of Adam's sin is that we stand condemned. "One trespass led to condemnation for all men" (Rom. 5:18). "For the judgment following one trespass brought condemnation" (v. 16). Paul is saying here that all people stand condemned, or guilty, in God's sight because of Adam's one sin that has become ours in union with Adam. We are liable to God's just sentence of condemnation because, on account of our union with Adam, his "one trespass" is reckoned to us.

The third forensic consequence of Adam's sin is that we are brought under the reign of death. "Death reigned from Adam to Moses" (Rom. 5:14). "Because of one man's trespass, death reigned through that one man" (v. 17). Death, we have seen, is the just penalty for sin. Here, Paul portrays death as a king with unchecked power over his subjects. We are helpless to extract ourselves from the reign of death.

Is it possible for us to find relief from our predicament through the law? Paul answers decidedly in the negative: "The law came in to increase the trespass" (Rom. 5:20). Paul assumes here that those who have been reckoned guilty of Adam's one sin have also come to love sin and willingly to be devoted to the service of sin. For such people, all that the law can do is worsen their sinful condition. In other words, as sinners, we can only take the law and make it an instrument in our sinful hands of sinning further. The problem, Paul stresses here and elsewhere, is not the law (Rom. 7:14). The problem is us. We take the good gift of God (His law) and put it to sinful use.

---

5  Most recent translations (NIV, NASB, ESV) render the verb in Romans 5:19 as "made." That translation is not incorrect but it is imprecise. As many commentaries observe, the Greek verb underlying that translation is more precisely rendered "constitute."

We may summarize Paul's teaching about Adam, sin, and humanity in Romans 5:12–21 along four lines. First, all human beings (with the exception of Christ) are in Adam. Adam is the representative head of all his posterity descended from him by ordinary generation. Second, the one sin of our representative, Adam, has been imputed or transferred to us. Third, we are therefore responsible for that one sin. We are counted sinners in Adam. We are condemned before God. We exist under the reign of death, the penalty of sin. Fourth, we are powerless to extract ourselves from this condition. We might look to the law to deliver us or to give us relief, but the law cannot rescue sinners from their plight.

## Lessons for Today

What lessons does Paul's teaching about sin have for us today? Three implications are apparent. First, when we, as believers, share the gospel with unbelievers, we know more about them than they know about themselves. Apart from Christ, every human being is guilty in Adam, condemned, and under the reign of death. The helps to which they look, such as the law, only end up aggravating their condition. They never make it better or cure it. Our goal as faithful witnesses to Christ is to show them from the Scripture the truth about them. It is not often easy for a person to come to the conclusion that he is God's enemy and not His friend, that he has a deep-rooted problem that is beyond his or any other creature's ability to solve. Even so, we must help such a person, through our witness and prayers, see himself in the way that God sees him. Unbelievers need to take in the bad news about themselves if the good news is to resonate with them at all.

Second, Paul's teaching about sin helps us put human divisions in proper perspective. We live in a world (as Paul did) that is marked by division. People are divided by many things—language, race, ethnicity, class, culture, national boundaries, political affiliations, and many other factors. Unbelieving people often recognize these divisions, lament over them, and seek to overcome them. Paul's gospel comes to us with startling news. In reality, human beings have something in common that runs more deeply than these many divisions. What unites people is their sinful solidarity in Adam. For Paul, to be "in Adam" is a more basic statement of our humanity in its present condition than to be a Jew or a Gentile. For this reason, Paul can issue a sweeping indictment of all human beings, whether Jew or Gentile, concluding as he does in Romans 3:9: "For we have already charged that all, both Jews and Greeks, are under sin." While the manifestations of our Adamic condition may vary from place to place, from culture to culture, from age to age, and from person to person, we all share in the same plight by nature—we are counted sinners in Adam, condemned, and under the reign of death. Any adequate reckoning with the human condition must take this reality into consideration.

Third, Paul's teaching about sin leaves us with an assessment that is bleak but not, in the final analysis, hopeless. To be sure, there is no hope to be found within Adamic humanity. All human religions and philosophies are expressions of the problem; they are not the solution. Neither is there hope for Adamic humanity in the law of God, even though the law of God is righteous and good.

Hope for human beings lies outside Adamic humanity. It is found only in the second Adam, Jesus Christ. As we shall see, the gospel of Christ is tailored precisely to our need and problem as sinners in Adam. How can Christ be the sinner's only hope? Only because He is descended from Adam but is not in Adam. As to His humanity, He is descended from Adam. But He is not the ordinary product of the union of Joseph and Mary. He was conceived by the Holy Spirit in the womb of the Virgin Mary and born of her. Jesus, therefore, is not in Adam even though He is truly human. If Jesus is not the Son of God who took on our true humanity while remaining outside Adam, He would be fallen as we are and could not save us. He needed to be a true and sinless man and He also at the same time had to be fully God in order to secure and provide the effective salvation that is available only outside of Adamic humanity. Any "Jesus" less than fully divine and fully human cannot help Adamic humanity.

What, then, is it that Christ has done to rescue, recover, and restore sinners? How has He undone what Adam has done? How has He done what Adam has failed to do? And how does all of this intersect with our lives? We are now prepared to hear Paul's gospel solution to our human plight.

Chapter 6

# PAUL'S GOSPEL—
# JUSTIFICATION (I)

We now come to the "crown jewel" of the gospel—justification by faith alone. John Calvin called it "the main hinge on which religion turns."[1] Martin Luther said of it, "If the article of justification is lost, all Christian doctrine is lost at the same time."[2]

There is, of course, more to Paul's gospel than justification by faith alone. At the same time, there is never less to Paul's gospel than justification by faith alone. Extract justification by faith alone from the gospel, and we no longer have the gospel in its biblical integrity.[3]

The great hinge of Romans falls at 3:21: "But now the righteousness of God has been manifested apart from the law, although the Law and the Prophets bear witness to it." Martin Lloyd-Jones said of the opening words of this verse ("But now"), "There are no more wonderful words in the whole of

---

1  John Calvin, *Institutes of the Christian Religion*, ed. John T. McNeill, trans. Ford Lewis Battles (Philadelphia: Westminster John Knox, 1960), 1:726 (3.11.1).

2  Martin Luther, *Lectures on Galatians, 1535*, in *Luther's Works*, ed. Jaroslav Pelikan, vol. 26 (St. Louis: Concordia, 1962), 9.

3  Although we will not take the time to look at Paul's epistle to the Galatians, Paul's letter bears powerful testimony to this truth. Paul's opponents, the Judaizers, were trying to supplement the work of Christ with works done by human beings in obedience to God's law. According to the Apostle, such a teaching constitutes "a different gospel" (Gal. 1:6). To add to the work of Christ in the doctrine of justification in this respect is to destroy the gospel altogether.

Scripture than just these two words."[4] Why would Lloyd-Jones say that? Recall that from Romans 1:18–3:20, Paul has labored to argue that sinners lack the righteousness that God requires of human beings. Now, for the first time in this letter, Paul begins to describe the righteousness that God has accomplished in Christ and that He freely gives in the gospel to sinners (see Rom. 1:16–17).[5] What, then, is this righteousness? How does it come to be ours?

## The Gift of Righteousness

In order to understand the righteousness of which Paul begins again to speak in Romans 3:21, we may point to three words that Paul uses in Romans 3:21–26. These words lay out for us the glorious nature of this gift of righteousness to the sinner.

The first word is "redemption"—we "are justified by his grace as a gift, through the redemption that is in Christ Jesus" (Rom. 3:24). The concept of "redemption" has a venerable biblical background. God used this term to describe His deliverance of Israel from bondage in Egypt (Ex. 6:6; 2 Sam. 7:23). In Isaiah's prophecy, God often speaks of Himself as the Redeemer of His people, not only in view of what He has done for His people, but also in view of what He is going to do for them (Isa. 59:20). The word "redemption" surfaces again at this crucial juncture of Paul's argument.

What does it mean to redeem? It means, in brief, to deliver enslaved people by payment of a ransom. Thus far in his letter, Paul has dedicated several chapters to establishing the bondage of humanity to sin. Human beings are given over to sin and to the guilt that sin carries with it. In Romans 3:21–26, Paul declares that Jesus Christ has delivered us from that bondage. We are now free from sin's guilt. That deliverance has come with a payment that Jesus has made on our behalf. What is the payment that Jesus has made? It is His death on the cross. Elsewhere, Paul connects this redemption with the shedding of Jesus' blood on the cross such that we receive the forgiveness of sins (Eph. 1:7).

The second word that Paul uses in Romans 3:21–26 to help us understand the gift of God's righteousness is "propitiation." Jesus is the One

---

4 As cited by Douglas Moo, *The Epistle to the Romans*, New International Commentary on the New Testament (Grand Rapids, Mich.: Eerdmans, 1996), 221.

5 The phrase "the righteousness of God" appears effectively for the first time in Romans 3:21 since its first appearance in 1:16–17 (in 3:5 the phrase has a different meaning from both 1:16–17 and 3:21).

"whom God put forward as a propitiation by his blood" (Rom. 3:25). Coupled with the word "blood," the word "propitiation" puts us again in well-traveled biblical territory. This term has its background in the world of the Old Testament sacrificial system. "Blood" refers to the shedding of the sacrificial victim's lifeblood. The shedding of blood was the indicator that the sacrifice had been offered and that expiation or atonement had been made. These sacrifices were repeated and were ongoing reminders of the final and sufficient sacrifice that Jesus Christ would offer at the cross. By Jesus' shed blood, the sins of His people are covered and the penalty for their sin is paid.

"Propitiation" has in view something more. Propitiation is the turning aside or averting of wrath. We may recall that Paul opens his account of the human condition in Romans 1:18 by declaring that human beings have a wrath problem. That is to say, "the wrath of God is revealed from heaven against all ungodliness and unrighteousness of men." Part of our plight as unrighteous sinners is that we are justly subject to the righteous God's wrath. The sacrificial death of Jesus Christ ("blood"), Paul says in Romans 3:21–26, has the effect of turning aside the wrath of God from sinners. That is to say, those for whom Jesus died have not only had their sins atoned for, but they have also had the Father's wrath averted from them. Jesus has turned aside the wrath of God from His people because He exhaustively bore the wrath of God on their behalf at the cross.

Paul underscores here the initiative of the Father: "God put forward [His Son] as a propitiation by his blood" (Rom. 3:23). The Father did not reluctantly or under duress agree to set aside His own wrath against those for whom Jesus died. In other words, the Son did not compel the Father to do something that He did not want to do. On the contrary, the Father sent His Son, Jesus, into the world to die on the cross precisely so that Jesus might propitiate the Father's wrath. For this reason, we may have every confidence that there is no hidden or remaining reserve of wrath in the Father toward us.

The third word that Paul uses in Romans 3:21–26 to help us understand this gift of righteousness, and the word that will occupy us for the rest of this chapter, is "justified"—believers "are justified by his grace as a gift, through the redemption that is in Christ Jesus" (Rom. 3:24). If the background to redemption is ancient slavery and the background to propitiation is (broadly) the world of the Old Testament sacrifices, then the background to justification is the law court. In God's law court, the defendants are guilty sinners and the judge is the righteous God, who renders a verdict concerning the defendants.[6]

Some have argued that justification carries the idea of inward transformation. Justification is said to be partly renovative and to encompass, at least in part, the transformative work of grace within us.[7] This claim prompts us to ask precisely how Paul understands justification. One clue to its meaning is found in comparison with its antonym, or opposite:

> For the judgment following one trespass brought *condemnation*, but the free gift following many trespasses brought *justification* (Rom. 5:16, emphasis added)

> It is God who *justifies*. Who is *to condemn*? (Rom. 8:33–34, emphasis added)

The proper opposite of justification is condemnation. This pairing, which is not unique to Paul (see Prov. 17:15), confirms justification as a strictly forensic (that is, courtroom) reality. Just as condemnation is a legal declaration that one is guilty, so justification is a legal declaration that one is righteous. Justification, therefore, is a wholly forensic and nonrenovative grace.

What, then, does it mean to be declared righteous? What exactly is the import of that verdict? Paul tells us that justification has in view two inseparable realities. The first is the pardon of all our sins. To be declared righteous means that our sins are entirely forgiven. We see this dimension of justification in Romans 4:7–8: "Blessed are those whose lawless deeds are forgiven, and whose sins are covered; blessed is the man against whom the Lord will not count his sin."[8] Forgiveness is not partial. It does not cover

---

6  We should note here a particular challenge that the English language (and many other modern languages) sets before us. The verb "justify" and the noun "righteousness" do not look at all similar in English. In Greek, however, they are cognate. That is to say, they are from the same word family and point to the same idea, as verb and noun, respectively.

7  This view is, in broad terms, that of the Roman Catholic church, as reflected in the Canons and Decrees of the Council of Trent.

8  Paul's preface to this citation in Romans 4:7–8 tells us that this citation explains the meaning of God "count[ing] righteousness apart from works" (v. 6). Notice in the immediately preceding

only some of our sins, whether the less serious ones or the ones that we committed before becoming a believer. Paul tells the Colossians that God in Christ has "forgiven us all our trespasses" (Col. 2:13). The pardon that God issues in Christ to the sinner is a complete pardon that has all of the sins of a believer in view.

But there is a second element to being declared righteous—being reckoned righteous. We are not only forgiven, having the guilt of our sins remitted, but we are also accepted and accounted righteous. That is to say, God does not simply remove from our record what is objectionable (the guilt of our sin); He proceeds to put something in its place. We are not merely declared innocent; we are counted righteous.

On what basis does God count the sinner righteous? How can a just God "[justify] the ungodly" (Rom. 4:5)? The answer is that God's verdict or declaration is based upon the righteousness that He gives to the sinner in the gospel. We will think further in a moment about how that righteousness is given and received. For now, we may briefly reflect on exactly what that righteousness is. We have seen Paul argue in Romans 3:21–26 that it centers on the redemptive, sacrificial, propitiatory death of Christ on the cross. Christ has died as our substitute and sacrifice. He has paid the due penalty for our sins. As a result, when we come to be united with Him in His death, we benefit from that death in that our sins are forgiven.

But our problem is not only that we have transgressed the law. We have also failed to keep the law. Christ has not only made full satisfaction for sin on our behalf, but He has also perfectly obeyed the law for us. Christ has met *all* the obligations of the law for us.[9] When we are savingly united to Christ, we are united to the Righteous One and come to share in His obedience on our behalf. In justification, God does not clear our account of debt to Him and tell us to start over and do better this time. We are, rather, counted righteous for Christ's sake. From the moment the sinner is justified, God regards him as righteous in His courtroom.

---

verses Paul's concern with justification by faith apart from works (vv. 1–5). Paul understands these words from Psalm 32 to provide definition to the justification of which he has been speaking since Romans 3:21. Paul's choice of Abraham and David in the early verses of Romans 4 is striking for another reason: it tells us that this justification was a reality known and experienced by Old Testament saints.

9　In our next chapter, we will see Paul develop this point explicitly in Romans 5:12–21.

The righteousness of Christ, on the basis alone of which we are justified, therefore consists of two things. It consists, on the one hand, of the full satisfaction that Christ made to God's justice for our sins, and, on the other hand, of His perfect obedience to the law. It is this righteousness that fully meets our need as sinners who stand guilty and worthy of condemnation before God. It is this righteousness that alone can bring us from condemnation to justification. Paul calls it the "righteousness of God" in Romans because it is the righteousness that not only meets with God's approval but also, as we shall see, is the provision of God in the gospel.

We should also note that this declaration or verdict is a *permanent* verdict. That is to say, once God declares the sinner righteous, that verdict does not expire. Nor will God ever withdraw it. Nor can we forfeit that status. Nor can any creature in the cosmos rob us of this precious gift. Paul begins Romans 8 on precisely this note: "There is therefore now no condemnation for those who are in Christ Jesus" (Rom. 8:1). Once we have passed from condemnation to justification, in union with Christ Jesus, we have been brought into what has been called a state of justification. That is to say, the justified believer will never again fall into condemnation.[10]

A moment's reflection on the character of justification will help us to see this all-important point more clearly. Paul has been unfolding our plight in the opening chapters of Romans in light of the impending day of judgment and the outpouring of divine wrath upon sinners (Rom. 1:18; 2:1–11). Because Christ has obeyed, died, and been raised from the dead for us, we stand righteous before God. We are no longer subject to God's wrath. Our sins are forgiven. We are treated as those who have fully met the law's demands. For these reasons, the verdict—"justified"—that God has passed over us in Christ is nothing less than or other than the verdict of the last day.[11] All these considerations constrain us to conclude that, in a

---

10 This fact does not mean that true believers no longer commit sins, or that their sins are not worthy of divine judgment, or that they have no need to continue to bring their sins before God in repentance and faith in Jesus Christ. It is to say that, when we become conscious of our sins, we have every confidence of our Father's willingness to forgive us of those sins as we heed His command to confess those sins to Him and to seek mercy from Him on the basis of the finished work of His Son.

11 We may note, further, that Paul tells us at the conclusion of Romans 4 that Christ was "delivered up for our trespasses and raised for our justification" (v. 25). Jesus' resurrection was the Father's vindication of the righteous Jesus who was condemned on the cross for the trespasses of His people.

person's justification in Christ, the verdict of the last day has been brought definitively, finally, and irreversibly into the present.

It is for this reason that the biblical writers universally look to the last day as a thing hoped for and not dreaded. Paul, for instance, cries out to the Corinthians, "Maranatha!" (1 Cor. 16:22, ESV text note; the main text reads, "Our Lord, come!"). Believers, by definition, are those who "have loved [Christ's] appearing" at the last day (2 Tim. 4:8). How can imperfect people look forward to a day when the divine Judge, who searches human hearts, will judge people impartially and righteously? Only by trusting that for them, as believers, that verdict has already been rendered. In Christ, that verdict is "righteous." We therefore live our Christian lives in light of that certainty. We do not strive for a righteousness that we do not yet have and may never attain. We do not have a temporary righteousness that we might forfeit. Instead, we live in the light of our full and unbroken possession of the righteousness by which we enjoy in the present the vindication of the last day.

## How Christ's Righteousness Becomes Ours

We have given some thought to what, for Paul, the "righteousness" of justification is. Christ secured that righteousness in His death and resurrection. It is not, however, automatically or universally availing. It is offered in the gospel and may be refused (see Rom. 9:30–10:4). So, how does justifying righteousness effectively break into our lives? We may answer that question along two lines—once concerning the mode in which the righteousness becomes ours, and the other concerning the means by which it becomes ours.

What is the mode by which justifying righteousness becomes ours? Paul's answer is found in the word *imputation*. Although Paul himself does not use this word, it is true to Paul's teaching about justification. We were introduced to this word in the last chapter when we thought about how Adam's sin comes into the possession of his posterity: it is credited, reckoned, or accounted to them. In the same manner, Christ's righteousness is credited, reckoned, or accounted to the sinner when he believes in Christ

---

This vindication came as the Father brought Jesus, in His resurrection, decisively from death into the immortal life of the age to come. The resurrection, then, was both declarative and definitive. It was, in that sense, Jesus' justification. We may fairly conclude that the believer, justified in Christ, shares in that definitive verdict passed over Jesus in His resurrection.

for salvation. This type of transfer of righteousness is well suited to the divine courtroom, where God definitively justifies us, or declares us righteous. For this reason, we speak of the *imputed* righteousness of Christ for justification. Justifying righteousness is not infused or inwrought. It is not worked in us gradually and progressively. It is imputed to us definitively and at once.

Paul shows us that the righteousness of justification is imputed in Romans 4:5, where he says that God "justifies the ungodly." If God's verdict were based on an inwrought or infused righteousness, then we would encounter a problem in this verse. Those who are justified are said to be "ungodly." That is, their character and life have no bearing on this verdict. God does not justify them with an eye to what kind of people they are (or will become). Paul therefore excludes moral transformation from the domain of justifying righteousness. The righteousness by which the sinner is justified must be imputed.

Paul makes a similar point in Philippians 3:9. Here, Paul tells the Philippians that the justified believer does not possess "a righteousness of [his] own that comes from the law, but that which comes through faith in Christ, the righteousness from God that depends on faith." Notice the contrast between these two kinds of "righteousness"—there is one's own righteousness derived from the law, and there is that righteousness that comes from God. The righteousness by which we are justified is in no way secured by anything in us, Paul says. It comes, rather, "from God." It is not sourced from within.[12] It comes to us from without. It is not infused; it is imputed.

A concise and full statement of this truth occurs in 2 Corinthians 5:21: "For our sake he made him to be sin who knew no sin, so that in him we might become the righteousness of God." Paul speaks here of two parties. First, there is Jesus, "who knew no sin." That is, He had no experiential acquaintance with sin—He neither had a sinful nature nor did He commit sin. Second, there are Christians. Paul assumes here that Christians, unlike Jesus, know sin. There is in this verse what has been termed a "Great Exchange." On the one hand, "for our sake [God] made [Jesus] to be sin."

---

12 Even if this righteousness were one that a person accomplished with the assistance of divine grace, Paul's point still stands. A righteousness that is indebted in any respect to what one does in obedience to the law, with or without the help of grace, is thereby "one's own" and not "from God."

Paul is speaking of what took place at the cross. God laid the sin of His people on Jesus. He did so by imputation. Our sins were imputed or accounted to Jesus at the cross. God therefore treated Jesus as a sinner. On the other hand, "in [Jesus] we . . . become the righteousness of God." As our sins were imputed to Jesus, so His righteousness is imputed to us. In the same way that our sins were transferred to Jesus at the cross, His righteousness is transferred to us for justification. Our sin was not infused into Jesus at the cross but imputed to Him. Jesus' righteousness, therefore, is not infused into us for justification but imputed to us.

## Righteousness by Faith

What, then, is the means by which the righteousness of God becomes ours? We have seen that in justification, we are declared righteous. This declaration is based solely upon Christ's righteousness, which is imputed to us. One remaining piece in Paul's teaching about justification in Romans is the means by which we appropriate this righteousness. The sole means by which we receive Christ's righteousness for justification is faith. Paul is concerned to say that we are justified by faith. He is equally concerned to say that we are not justified by works of the law. This formulation (justified by faith and not by works of the law) raises the question of how we define faith and works in reference to justification.

One place where Paul addresses this question is Romans 4:4–5, a passage directly related to justification by faith (see Rom. 4:1–3). Paul first defines the term *works*: "Now to the one who works, his wages are not counted as a gift but as his due" (Rom. 4:4). Here, Paul tells us that works belong to the realm of the marketplace. He speaks of works in terms of one's "wage" or "due." When you work, your employer does not give you your paycheck as charity or as a gift. It is your due. He owes you that money. That is the frame of reference for what Paul terms "justification by works."

Faith, on the other hand, operates in an entirely different realm. "To the one who does not work but believes in him who justifies the ungodly, his faith is counted as righteousness" (Rom. 4:5). Faith is the categorical opposite of works; it is defined in terms of not working. There is, then, no room for the two to coexist in the sphere of justification. One may be justified either by faith or by works, but not justified by both faith and works. Furthermore, God "justifies the ungodly." So far as the verdict of justification is concerned, we are "ungodly." We bring no merit to the table, nothing that would put God in our debt. The verdict of justification has no basis in the life that we have lived, are living, or will live, even in the works that we do in the power of the Spirit. Rather, God justifies the one who "trusts him who justifies the ungodly."

Faith, or trust, Paul tells us, does not look into ourselves to find resources for justification. It looks outside ourselves to the God who alone justifies. It finds its resources in God alone. Justifying faith is, ultimately, an act of trust. Faith involves more than understanding intellectually who Christ is and what He has done for our justification. It involves more than assent to the truth of the gospel. In addition to these things, faith means putting one's trust in God and in His Son as He is offered in the gospel. In this way, through faith one receives Christ and His righteousness as they are offered in the gospel.

Grasping justifying faith in these terms helps us avoid some misunderstandings that have arisen in the church's history. Paul is not saying that we are justified because of our "trust" or our "faithfulness." Faith is not a substitute work. God does not accept our faith in lieu of the works of the law that we could not do because of sin. Nowhere in his letters, in fact, does Paul ever say that we are justified "because of faith." He consistently says that we are justified "*by* faith" or "*through* faith." Faith is never the ground or basis of our justification—Christ's righteousness alone is the ground or basis of our justification. Faith has no power or virtue to justify us. It is God who justifies us, and that through faith. When we use the phrase *justified by faith*, we should be clear to ourselves and others that it is God who justifies us, not our faithfulness or our believing. Faith is the instrument or means by which we receive Christ and His righteousness for our justification.

We should also see here that Paul recognizes no other instrument or means in our justification than faith. This fact explains why the Reformers insisted that we are justified by faith *alone*. All parties at the time of the Reformation agreed that Christians are justified by faith. The dividing line lay in the word *alone*. As we see from Romans 4:4–5, the Reformers were faithful to Paul in declaring that faith is the sole instrument of our justification.

Why, we may ask, are we justified by faith alone? Paul's exposition of Abraham's justification in Romans 4 provides an answer. Paul connects Abraham's faith with the glory of God (Rom. 4:20). Abraham's growing faith in the "promise of God" brought glory to God. This state of affairs,

Paul reasons in Romans 3:27, excludes "boasting," which Abraham did not do (Rom. 4:2). Anytime that justification finds its grounds in ourselves, the result is always boasting in the creature. But when justification finds its grounds outside ourselves, in the saving work of the Son of God alone, the proper response is to boast in God (see Rom. 11:33–36). In this way, justification by faith alone leads to the glory of God.

One further reason why justification by faith alone brings glory to God and precludes boasting in the creature is that we cannot even claim credit for faith. Faith is a gift of God to the undeserving sinner. We do not add faith to the work of Christ. Faith is part of what Christ gives us as the fruit of His saving work on our behalf. Paul teaches this point at Philippians 1:29: "It has been granted to you that for the sake of Christ you should not only believe in him but also suffer for his sake." Both suffering and faith are said to be the gifts of God ("it has been granted to you") to His people. Similarly, Paul tells the Ephesians, "By grace you have been saved through faith. And this is not your own doing; it is the gift of God" (Eph. 2:8). Commentators debate the referent of the "this" and the "it" in the last clauses of this verse. What is the "gift of God"? Likely, Paul has in mind the whole proposition at the beginning of this verse, "For by grace you have been saved through faith." The entirety of our salvation, inclusive of faith, is said to be the gracious gift of God and not at all our own doing. In this case, what is true of the whole is true of the parts. Faith is God's gift to His people and not at all their own doing.

Faith, then, is the sole means of the sinner's justification. It contributes nothing to the basis upon which the sinner is justified. But faith is not thereby inactive or idle. Faith is very active. Its activity in justification, however, is entirely that of reception. It only receives Christ as He is offered in the gospel and rests upon Him alone for justification. In this way, the sinner is justified and the justifying God is glorified.

## Lessons for Today

What lessons do these precious truths have for Christians today? We may note at least two. First, Christianity stands alone from all other religions in this respect. Other religions stress that one must perform in order to be accepted by God or the gods, to earn salvation, and so on. Christianity insists that Christ alone has done all that one needs to be accepted by the true and living God. The gospel does not tell us to do something to supplement this work of Christ. It tells us to receive and rest in this finished work. As the early twentieth-century Reformed theologian B.B. Warfield put the matter in another context, "We all enter the Kingdom of heaven . . . as little children *who do not do, but are done for.*"[13] "Do not do, but done for" is as fine a summary of this portion of Paul's teaching as one could desire. The beginning, middle, and end of the Christian life is that we stand forgiven and accepted as righteous, and that these realities rest solely upon the unshakable foundation of Christ and His righteousness.

Second, the truth of justification on account of the obedience of Christ received only by faith shows that the Christian life is one of faith, and not only at its beginnings. Paul can say about the ongoing Christian experience, "We walk by faith, not by sight" (2 Cor. 5:7). The Christian's mode of existence is "faith." Similarly, Paul can tell the Galatians, "And the life I now live in the flesh I live by faith in the Son of God, who loved me and gave himself for me" (Gal. 2:20). The whole of the Christian life, which is lived "*in* the flesh"—but never "*according* to the flesh"—is one of "faith," specifically faith in Christ "who loved me and gave himself for me."

Faith in Christ, then, is not a box to be checked and then set aside. It is not something from which we graduate to higher levels of spirituality and devotion. Whether the believer is young or old, new or mature, his life is defined, determined, and directed by faith. This faith is never retiring or passive. It is active and, we shall see, fruitful and bountiful. One lesson that no Christian can afford to forget is that Christian living finds an unparalleled motive in the work of Christ for our justification. To live the Christian life well, then, we must be growing in our sense of the love of Christ for us, especially His self-giving love for us at the cross. This growth happens through faith. Fruitful Christians are Christians who are growing in faith. Christians who grow in faith will be found often in the Word of God, drinking from the inexhaustible wells of the love of Christ at the cross. And, with faith growing stronger and stronger, we, like Abraham, will give all glory to God.

---

13 Benjamin B. Warfield, *Selected Shorter Writings,* ed. John E. Meeter (Phillipsburg, N.J.: P&R, 1970), 1:329. Emphasis added.

Chapter 7

# PAUL'S GOSPEL— JUSTIFICATION (II)

One of the first great lessons of the gospel in Romans is that the righteousness that sinners lack and need is the righteousness that God has accomplished in Christ and freely gives to all who believe. This free gift of righteousness forms the core of Paul's teaching on justification. God declares the sinner righteous on the sole basis of the righteousness of Christ. This righteousness is imputed to us and received through faith alone, apart from the works of the law.

Some have objected to this accounting of the Apostle's teaching in Romans. This explanation is said to involve God in what has been called a "legal fiction." That is to say, God by a mere declaration or "say-so" is said to call sinners what they are patently *not*—"righteous." What is this, it is argued, but verbal sleight of hand? The alternative is the position maintained at the time of the Reformation by the Roman Catholic Church. God declares a human being righteous only when he is inwardly, truly, and completely "righteous," and thus the responsibility of the believer is to continue to strive toward righteousness. Only in this way, it is said, will God's declaration correspond to reality.

How may we respond to this objection? How can believers reconcile this divine declaration with the ongoing reality of sin in their persons and lives? The avenue to answering both these questions from Paul's writings is "union with Christ." The bond between the sinner and Christ provides the framework within which Paul would have us understand our justification. This framework, which Paul addresses at length in Romans 5:12–21, enriches our understanding of the grace of justification and, in so doing, offers profound pastoral encouragement and support to believers.

After Paul completes his initial discussion of justification in Romans 3:21–31, he provides an extended reflection on Abraham (and David) as the paradigm of the sinner who is justified by faith alone in Christ alone (Rom. 4:1–25). In Romans 5:1–11, Paul rehearses the many benefits that are the lasting possession of the justified believer. It is in Romans 5:12–21 that Paul shows us the depths of the foundation upon which these benefits rest. We may explore two lines of Paul's teaching in these verses: first, that there is a union or bond between Christ and the believer, and second, what Christ has done for those who are united to Him.

## Union with Christ

In a previous chapter, we saw that Paul tells the Christians at Rome that there is a union between Adam and his posterity. Adam was not only a fully historical human being but also a representative man. That is to say, all human beings (Christ excepted) are united with Adam, their covenantal head. Adam's sin has come into their possession by imputation. They are therefore guilty of Adam's first sin. As such, all people in Adam are constituted sinners, condemned, and placed under the reign of death, the wage and penalty of sin.

We also have seen that Adam and Christ stand in parallel. Each is a representative man. Christ is the second Man, the last Adam (1 Cor. 15:45, 47). In Romans 5:12–21, Paul calls both Adam and Christ "one man" (Rom. 5:15, 17, 19). In light of this parallel, we expect there to be a representative union also between Christ and His people, and, in fact, there is such a union.

In Paul's discussion of this union or bond in Romans 5:12–21, we may first look at those whom Christ represents. Adam represents the entirety of the human race (Christ excepted). Whom does Paul say that Christ represents? In verse 18, Adam's sin is said to come into the possession of "all men" and Christ's work is also said to come into the possession of "all men." In verse 19, Paul changes his wording slightly. Adam's sin is said to render "the many" sinners, whereas Christ's work renders "the many" righteous.

Paul's wording has prompted some readers of Romans to ask whether the Apostle is teaching universalism, the doctrine that all human beings will be saved. When Paul says that "one act of righteousness leads to justification and life for *all men*" (Rom. 5:18, emphasis added), does this mean that Christ has accomplished the salvation of every human being?

There are at least two significant problems with saying that Paul advocates that kind of universalism. First, Paul elsewhere teaches that on the day of judgment, some human beings will be ushered from the final judgment to everlasting punishment. Jesus, Paul writes, will "[inflict] vengeance on those who do not know God and on those who do not obey the gospel of our Lord Jesus. They will suffer the punishment of eternal destruction, away from the presence of the Lord and from the glory of his might, when he comes on that day to be glorified in his saints, and to be marveled at among all who have believed" (2 Thess. 1:8–10). Paul has in mind here two overlapping groups of people. First, there are those who "do not know God." While intellectually aware of the existence and of certain attributes of God (see Rom. 1:18–32), they do not receive this knowledge with approval and delight. Second, some of these people have also heard the gospel and have refused to "obey" it. That is to say, they have refused Christ's summons to repent and believe in Him for salvation.

When these people appear before Christ on the day of judgment, He will pronounce sentence on them and proceed to punish them. Paul describes that scene graphically. Jesus will "inflict vengeance on them" (2 Thess. 1:8). They will "suffer the punishment of eternal destruction" (2 Thess. 1:9). The just judgment that Jesus inflicts on those who remain in their sins when they appear before Him is a punishment that will endure forever.[1] At the same time, they will be cast away from His presence, that is, His favorable presence. Christ's people, along with the holy angels, alone will enjoy that blessed presence. The damned will be in the presence of Christ forever, but that presence will be one of wrath and just indignation. In summary, the wicked are both deprived of the eternal bliss and glory that the redeemed will enjoy with Christ forever and must endure eternal punishment in hell. Such teaching cannot be reconciled with the doctrine that Christ has saved every human being.

---

1 In chapter 12, we will discuss in more detail what Paul has to say about the future of humanity, both believers and unbelievers.

A second problem with the doctrine of universalism is that it is not faithful to Paul's teaching in Romans 5:18–19. Notice that Paul shifts from the word "all" in verse 18 to the word "many" in verse 19. That shift is our first clue to the fact that what Paul has in mind by "all" is something other than the entirety of the human race without exception. A further clue comes when we remember that when Paul defined the word "all" in relation to Adam, the Apostle did not there mean the entirety of the human race without exception. The reason we may confidently say so is because there is one human being who is not included in Adam, namely, the man Christ Jesus. We must define the word "all" in relation to Adam in terms of "all the human beings whom Adam represents." (In Adam's case, this amounts to every human being ordinarily descended from Adam.) The same definition of "all" must apply to Christ in verse 18. When Paul says "one act of righteousness leads to justification and life for all men," he is referring to all the human beings whom Jesus represents. How many or how few are in that group is not Paul's concern in this verse. In any case, Paul does not teach in verses 18–19 that every human being will be saved in Jesus Christ.

The question remains for us, however, as to why Paul speaks in the manner that he does. Paul has good reason to use the word "all" and to use it in precisely this place. The word "all" has already shown up in important places in Paul's argument in Romans. In Romans 1:16, the thesis of his letter, Paul says that the gospel "is the power of God for salvation to *everyone* who believes" (emphasis added). In the Greek, the word "everyone" is the same word that is translated "all" in Romans 5:18. In Romans 3:9, summarizing his indictment of humanity, the Apostle concludes, "We have already charged that *all*, both Jews and Greeks, are under sin" (emphasis added). In Romans 3:22–23, describing the reach and scope of God's gift of righteousness to sinners, Paul speaks of "the righteousness of God through faith in Jesus Christ for *all* who believe. For there is no distinction: for *all* have sinned and fall short of the glory of God" (emphasis added). That is to say, the gift of righteousness is designed to meet the need of every human sinner. No sinner can say of this gift that it does not suit him or address his plight. The paradigmatic example of the justified believer is Abraham, "the father of *all* who believe without being circumcised" (Rom. 4:11, emphasis added).

In Romans, Paul breaks down the understanding of the Jew/Gentile distinction held by many Jews in his day. Jewishness, Paul has argued, does not get one closer to God. Neither does the mere fact of being a Gentile exclude one from being saved. In fact, Paul argues, there is a more basic distinction than that of Jew and Gentile. It concerns whether one is in Adam or in Christ. These two representative heads encompass the entirety of the human race. The core identity and destiny of every human being, whatever his ethnicity, is determined by this relation. In this way, Paul underscores how desperate the human condition is apart from Christ, even as he helps believers marvel at the reach and depth of God's grace in Christ. Christ's work is for all kinds of sinners, without regard to the divisions that so often characterize human interactions. The reach of Christ's grace is deeper and wider than we can imagine.

## What Christ Has Done

There is, then, a union or bond between Christ and His people. He is their representative head. What is it that Christ has done for those who are united to Him? Answering that question is Paul's chief concern in Romans 5:12–21. We may summarize his teaching in these verses along three lines. First, Paul again brings us into the courtroom of God: "And the free gift is not like the result of that one man's sin. For the judgment following one trespass brought condemnation, but the free gift following many trespasses brought justification" (v. 16). Adam's "trespass" led to "condemnation." The "free gift," however, resulted in a different verdict in God's courtroom, namely, "justification." In verses 18–19, we see Paul continuing to use legal language ("condemnation . . . justification"; "constituted sinners . . . constituted righteous"; author's translation). Paul's concern in this portion of Romans is not a change that is wrought within us but a new status or standing bestowed upon us.

Second, Paul explains Christ's work in Romans 5:12–21 in terms of imputation. Just as Adam's sin was imputed to us in God's courtroom and resulted in our condemnation, so Christ's work is imputed to us in God's courtroom and results in our justification. Paul attributes our justification to "the free gift" (v. 16). When we come into possession of that "free gift," we are declared righteous. It is "the free gift by the grace of that one man Jesus Christ" (v. 15). Our representative head, Christ Jesus, in grace and mercy secures a gift for His people. In view of that gift alone we are justified before God. Paul tells us in verse 18 what that "free gift" consists of: "One act of righteousness leads to justification and life for all men." Christ's "righteousness" is given to us and we are therefore declared righteous (justified) on the sole basis of that gift. Paul then says in verse 19, "By the one man's obedience the many will be constituted righteous" (author's translation). In these verses (16, 18–19), Paul makes clear that our justification in Christ is grounded entirely and exclusively upon the free gift of Christ's righteousness. This free gift becomes ours by imputation. Just as Adam's sin was imputed to us for condemnation, Christ's righteousness is imputed to us for justification.

Third, Paul tells us in Romans 5:12–21 about the free gift of Christ's righteousness. What precisely is delivered to the person who is united to Christ such that this person is justified by God? Paul calls this gift Jesus' "one act of righteousness" (v. 18) and His "obedience" (v. 19). Certainly, in this righteousness and obedience Paul must have in mind the death of Jesus Christ on the cross. As we have seen Paul argue in Romans 3:21–26, Jesus' sacrificial death is the centerpiece of the believer's "righteousness." Furthermore, Paul tells the Philippians, Jesus was "obedient to the point of death, even death on a cross" (Phil. 2:8). Certainly, Jesus' death on the cross was His crowning act of obedience to the Father.

But when Paul speaks of Jesus' "obedience" in Romans 5:19, he has in mind more than the cross. He is thinking of the whole life of obedience that Jesus undertook and accomplished on behalf of His people. Not only Jesus' sacrificial death but also His perfect life of obedience is credited to the sinner for justification.

What are the indications that Paul is thinking along these lines in this section of Romans? One is that Paul stresses the superabundance of what Christ has done in comparison with Adam's work. If death has reigned through Adam, "much more" will Christ's justified people "reign in life through the one man Jesus Christ" (Rom. 5:17). "Where sin increased, grace abounded all the more" (v. 20). Jesus has not merely undone what Adam did. That is to say, He has not simply returned His people to the place of pre-fallen Adam in the garden, giving them a second chance to win confirmed, eternal life through obedience.

How do we know this, and what exactly has Jesus the last Adam done for His people that Adam did not do? The contrast that Paul establishes in Romans 5:17 answers these questions. Adam's one sin has resulted in "death" for humanity. Adam, of course, had been threatened with death for disobedience (Gen. 2:16–17). Implied is the fact that Adam's obedience would have secured "life"—confirmed life, consummate life, the life of everlasting communion and fellowship with God. But Adam failed to do this. What Adam failed to do, Christ has done. Therefore, Paul says that we not only receive "the free gift of righteousness," but we also will "reign in life through the one man Jesus Christ" (Rom. 5:17). Christ has won life for us, and in Him we will be given entrance into the reign of life. Further, it is in view of the "free gift of righteousness" that we will, in Christ, "reign in life." The gift of righteousness does not return us to the place of pre-fallen Adam in the garden of Eden. It takes us to the place where Adam should have gone but did not, to the place where the obedient Son of God did in fact go—eternal life.

The righteousness of justification, then, is our title to eternal life. This is so because the gift of righteousness includes more than Jesus' death on the cross, which canceled the guilt and penalty of our sins and averted the wrath of God from us. This gift of righteousness also includes Jesus' life of obedience. Jesus has fully obeyed the law on our behalf and has therefore won the life that perfect law-keeping merits (see Rom. 10:5; Gal. 3:12). Our entrance into eternal life is not suspended upon our best efforts. It is freely given to us because our representative head, Christ, has earned it for us in His life and death. It is for these reasons that Paul can begin this chapter by saying to believers, "Since we have been justified by faith . . . we rejoice in hope of the glory of God" (Rom. 5:1–2).

## Lessons for Today

What lessons do we learn from Paul's teaching about justification in Romans? We may point to at least two. First, Paul is well aware that we live in a world fractured by divisions of language, culture, race, gender, and religion, to name only a few. Sometimes these divisions are occasioned by legitimate differences in our created humanity under the providence of God (whether we are male or female; whether we speak English or Korean). Sometimes these divisions directly spring from sin (false religions, for instance). The world responds to these divisions in very different ways. Sometimes, the world tries to make these divisions ultimate—the source of our deepest identity, that which provides meaning and direction for our lives. At other times, the world vainly looks for ways to try to overcome these divisions and to pursue some kind of unity that transcends our differences.

Paul approaches our divisions in another way entirely. He does not ask that his readers cease to be Jewish or Gentile people. What he does instead is show us that the deepest truth about our humanity is found in our relationship with one of two people—Adam or Christ. If we are in Adam, we stand in sinful solidarity with all other human beings in Adam. Paul reminds us in this portion of his argument that in Adam, we all stand equally condemned and that death reigns over us all. It is a grim reminder of our human condition apart from the saving grace of Christ.

But if we are in Christ, this relationship and all that it carries are due entirely to the gracious initiative of God. The words "grace" and "gift" course like a river through Romans 5:12–21. Paul wants us to understand that at no point in our Christian lives—beginning, middle, or end—may we claim any credit. We are entirely indebted to God's grace. By grace, we have been given title to a new reign (life) and have joined a new people (those who are in Christ with us). Therefore, for all our differences, the people of God are all one in Christ. No other people, nation, or organization can claim this kind of unity. Our unity rests on nothing in ourselves, but entirely on our Savior and what He has done to rescue us from sin and death and bring us to eternal life. These realities should transform the way that we think about our relationships with fellow believers and our life within the church.

The second lesson we learn from Paul's teaching on justification is how wide-ranging the grace of justification is. Justification is our title to eternal life, the life in which we shall reign. Justification, in fact, makes us to "reign in life" (Rom. 5:17) because by it we receive life that can never be forfeited. We have a certain, glorious future and, therefore, hope for the present.

Paul does not leave this reality a matter of abstraction or speculation. He wants us to understand it in concrete and practical terms. This burden is one that Paul shoulders in Romans 5:1–11. What does it mean to be justified and given a title to eternal life? It means that "we have peace with God through our Lord Jesus Christ"—we are no longer at enmity with God, and we are now in a relationship of wholeness and well-being with Him (v. 1). This is so because we have been reconciled to God by the work of Christ, whom God sent in love for us, His enemies (vv. 6–7, 10–11). It means that we now "stand" through faith in "this grace" of justification (v. 2). Not even "sufferings" can rob us of this great gift (v. 3). In fact, "sufferings" are God's appointed means of working in us "hope" (vv. 3–5). The trials of life, therefore, do not proceed from God's wrath toward us but from His love, which the Spirit supplies to us in greater and greater measure (v. 5; see also v. 8). In all this, God is ushering us toward what Paul calls "the glory of God," which is our "hope" and in which we now "rejoice" (v. 2).

These realities all rest on the finished work of Christ, and that work is our possession in unbreakable union with Christ. The gospel, therefore, gives us a firm anchor for the soul. When we are in trial or distress, when we are perplexed, when we are abandoned or lonely—in whatever circumstances we find ourselves—what Christ has done for us and is now doing in our lives is balm for the soul. Far from being an antiquated or forgotten event in the remote past of our Christian life, justification speaks audibly into our present and points us to that future day when we shall certainly see our glorious Savior face-to-face.

Chapter 8

___

# PAUL'S GOSPEL—
# SANCTIFICATION (I)

We have thus far looked at two major planks of Paul's presentation of the gospel in Romans. The first is human sin. Sin is the great presupposition of the gospel message. Sin has occasioned the salvation that only the gospel offers to human beings. The second plank is justification. The grace of justification is a definitive and irreversible change of relation in God's courtroom. Sinners, though deserving of condemnation, are declared righteous by God. Through faith in Christ, their sins are fully pardoned and they are accepted and accounted righteous in God's sight. This legal declaration is not owing to any change in them. It is based solely upon Christ's righteousness, imputed to them and received through faith alone.

Paul, however, is hardly done presenting the fullness of the riches of the gospel of grace. Christ delivers His people not only from the guilt and penalty of sin but also from the dominion, presence, and power of sin. The gospel involves, therefore, a complete rescue operation from sin. We are not partially delivered and then instructed to finish the job. Christ is a full and sufficient Savior from sin.

Beginning in Romans 6, Paul shows us how Christ has delivered us from the dominion of sin and is progressively freeing us from its presence and power. Paul uses a word in this chapter to describe this ongoing work of Christ: "sanctification" (Rom. 6:19, 22). If justification deals with the legal dimensions of our sin, then sanctification deals with the enslaving and corrupting dimensions of our sin. For this reason, Paul's discussion of "righteousness" in this chapter (see Rom. 6:13, 16, 18–20) differs from that of Romans 3:21–5:21. The "righteousness" in view in Romans 6 does not concern the courtroom, as it has in previous chapters. It concerns, rather, the character of our lives—our thinking, choosing, and behaving.

This renovative work of grace is Paul's leading concern in Romans 6–8, and it is the subject of each of our next three chapters as well. In this chapter, we will look at Romans 6.

Our study of Romans 6 begins by considering how Paul concludes his argument in Romans 5. In Romans 5:20–21, he writes, "Where sin increased, grace abounded all the more, so that, as sin reigned in death, grace also might reign through righteousness leading to eternal life through Jesus Christ our Lord." Paul tells us here that we have been brought from the reign of sin (see Rom. 5:14, 17) into the superabundant reign of grace.

As he opens Romans 6, Paul is concerned to avoid a misunderstanding of what he has said at the end of Romans 5, so he gives voice to that misunderstanding in Romans 6:1: "What shall we say then? Are we to continue in sin that grace may abound?" The Apostle's answer is decisive: "By no means!" (Rom. 6:2). The gospel does not call us to pursue sin in the interests of increasing grace. The gospel does not paint vice in the colors of virtue. The gospel is not a divine license to sin.

How, then, does the gospel speak to the dominion and presence of sin in the lives of human beings? In Romans 6, Paul helps us see the resources, found in Christ alone, that address these dimensions of sin. He does so in two ways. First, he shows us a uniquely Christian mind. Second, he shows us uniquely Christian mandates.

## The Christian Mind

For Paul, renewal or sanctification in the Christian life involves both the mind and behavior. But sanctification must start with the mind. This is Paul's point a little later in Romans: "Do not be conformed to this world, but be transformed by the renewal of your mind, that by testing you may discern what is the will of God, what is good and acceptable and perfect" (Rom. 12:2).[1] There

---

1 The Christian "nonconformity" that Paul has in mind here concerns "the world." Recall from our discussion in chapter 3 that "the world," for Paul, is often interchangeable with "the present evil

is, then, a Pauline priority of knowing over doing. What is it that we are to know? In chapter 6, Paul shows us that the Christian has an identity that is all his own. There are things that are true by definition of each and every actual Christian. These realities must be known, believed, and then acted upon.

We may point to at least two basic realities in particular that surface throughout this chapter. The first is that in Christ, the believer is dead to sin. Paul first asserts this claim at Romans 6:2: "How can we who died to sin still live in it?" Paul is not issuing a command ("Die to sin!"). Neither is he pointing to something that lies in our future ("You will, one day, die to sin"). He is, rather, stating a fact of our existence, one that lies in our past. The believer is dead to sin.

What does it mean to be "dead to sin"? Crucially for Paul, the believer is dead to sin by virtue of his being in saving union with Christ: "If we have been united with him in a death like his" (Rom. 6:5); "we have died with Christ" (Rom. 6:8). According to Paul, we who are united with Christ have died to sin because Christ Himself has died to sin. This is Paul's astonishing claim at Romans 6:10, which states, "For the death he died he died to sin, once for all." Paul is not saying here that Jesus was sinful and overcame His personal sin at the cross. Paul elsewhere affirms the sinlessness of Jesus who "knew no sin" (2 Cor. 5:21; see Rom. 8:3; Phil. 2:7). Paul is saying that what Jesus did in dying to sin, He did for His people. Jesus' once-for-all death on the cross for His people brought about a decisive victory over sin. What kind of victory did Christ accomplish? As Paul's argument goes on to show, Jesus' death on the cross nullifies the dominion of sin over His people. When the sinner is united to Christ, he comes to share in all that Jesus has won for us in His death (and resurrection). This victory includes the defeat of sin as an enslaving power.

For this reason, Paul commands believers to "consider [them]selves dead to sin and alive to God in Christ Jesus" (Rom. 6:11). He reminds the church, "Sin will have no dominion over you" (v. 14). We "have been brought from death" (v. 13) and "set free from sin," that is, its lordship and dominion (v. 7).[2] These are realities that the believer is liable to forget and

---

age" (Gal. 1:4). Christians are not to be morally conformed to the sinful patterns of thinking and living that characterize unbelief.

2   The verb that Paul uses in this verse is the same verb that is elsewhere translated in his correspondence "justify." Here, Paul is neither talking about the grace of justification nor is he confusing the

must therefore keep in the forefront of his thinking. Paul is not saying that we summon these realities into existence by thinking about them. On the contrary, these realities are true of every genuine believer regardless of what he is doing, thinking, or feeling at any given moment. Paul wants us to appropriate these realities into our day-to-day existence. That appropriation begins by setting our minds on the once-for-all, unrepeatable work of Christ for us at the cross.

In Romans 6:6, Paul helps us better understand the connection between this new relationship with sin and the lamentable but persistent presence of sin in our lives: "We know that our old man was crucified with him in order that the body of sin might be brought to nothing, so that we would no longer be enslaved to sin."[3] Who or what is the "old man" here? There is a clear connection between the word "man" here and the word "man" as Paul has used it of Adam in Romans 5:12–21. The "old man" describes who we once were in Adam, specifically, who were under the dominion and bondage of sin. This "old man" was "crucified with [Jesus]" at the moment when, being savingly united to Christ, we came to share in the work of Christ on the cross for us. Who we once were has been, as it were, nailed to the cross of Christ. The result is that we are no longer "enslaved to sin." Further, our "body of sin," that is, our whole self as determined and governed by sin, has been nullified.[4]

The believer has not only died to sin; the second basic reality that runs through Romans 6 is that in Christ, the believer has also been raised unto life. We have been united to Christ not only in His death but also in His resurrection: "We shall certainly be united with him in a resurrection like his" (Rom. 6:5). Paul is not speaking of a purely future reality for the Christian. He is speaking of something that we presently experience and enjoy. When

---

graces of justification and sanctification. Rather, he is saying that believers have made a clear and decisive break with the lordship of sin. United to Christ, believers have a brand-new relationship with sin and with holiness.

3  Following the ESV text note. The ESV text renders the phrase "old self." The ESV text's rendering is accurate but obscures the connection between this phrase and Paul's use of the same word "man" in Rom. 5:12–21.

4  The phrase "body of sin" does not refer to a part of the human person, as though there may be some other part of one's humanity untouched by sin. The phrase refers to the fact that sin once determined the entirety of who we used to be, and that this reality came to expression in our physical bodies.

Paul says that we "have been brought from death to life" (Rom. 6:13), he is referring to *resurrection* life (see also Eph. 2:5–6; Col. 3:1–4). To be sure, we await the resurrection of the body at the last day (see 1 Cor. 15). This fact does not mean that we now have no share in the resurrection. Paul tells us that we have already begun to share in the resurrection.

In what sense, then, is the resurrection a present reality for the believer? Paul speaks of this reality in the context of the believer's union with Christ. To understand our present resurrection life, we must first understand something about Christ's own resurrection. In Romans 6:9, Paul tells us, "We know that Christ, being raised from the dead, will never die again; death no longer has dominion over him." The resurrection marked Jesus' decisive breach with the reign or "dominion" of death. Having submitted Himself to the power of death in His death (and burial), He burst the bonds of death in His resurrection. He was raised immortal, never to die again. His voluntary submission to death and its power was complete and concluded, and death stood vanquished. Further, Paul says, "the life he lives he lives to God" (Rom. 6:10). At the resurrection, the man Jesus entered into a sphere of resurrection life, never to leave. What is said to define or qualify this resurrection life here is that it is a life lived unto God.[5]

How does Christ's resurrection affect the Christian? When people are savingly united to Christ, they also are brought out of the sphere determined by death and ushered into the sphere determined by (resurrection) life ("[we] have been brought from death to life"; Rom. 6:13). In short, we "live with him," that is, the resurrected Jesus (Rom. 6:8). We are therefore "alive to God in Christ Jesus" (Rom. 6:11). We share in Christ's resurrection no less than in His death. We have not only a brand-new relationship with sin but also a brand-new relationship with holiness and righteousness, the characteristic features of this resurrection life.

In summary, Paul teaches the believer to cultivate a mind-set that is uniquely Christian. This mind-set consciously and regularly reflects on the fact that Jesus, in His death and resurrection, died to sin and rose to life for

---

5   This expression should not be taken to mean that Jesus did not live His life unto God before the resurrection. Paul is saying here that the characteristic of this new sphere of resurrection of life is that it is thoroughly oriented to and determined by God. It is this characteristic that he wants to impress upon believers' thinking. What has changed for Jesus is that He no longer lives in a realm characterized by sin and death and is no longer subject to the dominion of death (Rom. 6:9–10).

us. When we are savingly united to Christ by the Spirit, and through faith, we immediately share in the resources of His death and resurrection. We have a new relationship with sin—the dominion or reign of sin has been broken in our lives. We are no longer enslaved and determined by sin. We have a new relationship with righteousness—a new dominion or reign has replaced that of sin. We are under the reign of life or "grace" (Rom. 6:14). It is not enough for Paul that these things are true of the believer. The believer must make a point of "consider[ing]" them (Rom. 6:11).

## The Christian Mandate

Adopting and nurturing this mind-set is a crucial first step in making progress in the Christian life.[6] We cannot expect to do well in combating sin and pursuing holiness if we are not heeding Paul at this point. But we must never think that the project of sanctification is purely a mental exercise. For Paul, there are also concrete actions that we must take. Grasping who we are in Christ must lead to corresponding action. God has assigned us a role to play in this, His gracious work. We have a job to do.

The danger that the Christian faces is to err on one of two extremes. The first is what we have just described above. We make sanctification a purely mental exercise with no corresponding action. The second is that we make sanctification a purely behavioral exercise wherein all we must do is obey a set of rules and refrain from certain actions. We may even view our efforts here as our own unaided response to what God has done for us in our justification. The first view sees our ongoing sanctification as something that God does to us, independent of any effort on our part. The second view sees sanctification as something that we do for God, independent of any assisting grace on His part.

Both of these approaches to the Christian life, however common they are in the church, are grossly defective. In Romans 6, Paul gives us a balanced approach that avoids these extremes. We have thus far traced what has been termed the "indicative" of the Christian life—that which is now true of us in Christ, through faith. We now turn to what has been termed the "imperative" of the Christian life—wherein we take up commands that

---

6  I am indebted in the discussion that follows to the reflections of Gaffin, *By Faith, Not by Sight*, 77–85.

are obligatory and nonnegotiable. Paul does not ask us whether we would like to keep them. These commands are an expected and necessary part of the pattern of Christian living.

Paul never separates the indicative and the imperative. Even where one goes unstated, it is always assumed and implied when the other is mentioned. In Romans 6, Paul yokes the two inseparably together. We cannot have one without the other. Further, Paul places the two in a set and irreversible order—the indicative always has priority over the imperative.[7] That is to say, it is a matter of first importance to Paul to point us back to what is true of us in Christ and to the resources for obedience that are ours through faith in Christ. These realities make up the context within which the Apostle issues commands to believers. In this sense, the imperative of the Christian life is a matter of grace. Furthermore, the goal or outcome of the imperatives is "eternal life" (Rom. 6:22), which Paul tells us is "the free gift of God . . . in Christ Jesus our Lord" (Rom. 6:23). From start to finish, Paul reminds us, the Christian life is the life of grace.

With this basic framework in place, we are now poised to think about the *mandates* that must accompany and follow the *mind-set* that Paul has been fostering in Romans 6. We may latch onto two words from this chapter that help us grasp the breadth and depth of the reach of grace in transforming our lives. These two key words are "slave" and "submit."

Paul would have us think of ourselves as "slaves of God" (Rom. 6:22). In antiquity, a slave was someone whose life and destiny were utterly controlled and determined by his master.[8] Why does Paul use this graphic image of the Christian, especially when he elsewhere describes the Christian life as one of "freedom" (see Gal. 5:1, 13; 2 Cor. 3:17)? Paul may well be aware that this question arises in our minds, for he notes, "I am speaking in human terms, because of your natural limitations" (Rom. 6:19) That is, he is appealing to something familiar to his first-century readers while recognizing that this image is hardly a comprehensive way of capturing the Christian life. Even so, there is a truth here that Paul wants us to grasp.

---

7  Gaffin, *By Faith, Not by Sight*, 81.

8  It is important to distinguish first-century servitude from the race-based chattel slavery that characterized the modern West into the nineteenth century. The two are sufficiently different that it is inaccurate and inappropriate to draw conclusions about slavery in antiquity from modern practices of slavery.

Paul first makes the startling claim that every human being is a slave: "You are slaves of the one whom you obey, either of sin, which leads to death, or of obedience, which leads to righteousness" (Rom. 6:16). It is in our humanity to serve. The question is not whether we will serve; it is whom or what we will serve. Adamic humanity is in the service of sin—they are "slaves of sin" (v. 20)—and the outcome of that service is "death," that is, eternal death (see vv. 21, 23). In Christ, we have been made "slaves of God" (v. 22) or "slaves of righteousness" (v. 18). Our former service has been broken, and a new service has been established. We now serve what we once hated, and we now hate what we once served. This service, likewise, bears "fruit," namely, "sanctification" and, ultimately, "eternal life" (v. 22). Since "eternal life" is "the free gift of God . . . in Christ Jesus our Lord," our servitude, we must never forget, is all of grace (v. 23).

Paul, then, wants every believer to see himself as a slave of God. The believer has been rescued from his former master, sin. He has been brought into the wholesome service of a new Master, with a promising future. What defines his existence is not autonomy or self-direction. What defines his existence is the will of his master. What should please the slave is what pleases the master.

That every believer is a slave leads naturally to Paul's second key word, "submit" (ESV "present"). The hallmark of a slave is his submission to his master. This reality informs Paul's reasoning in Romans 6:16:

> Do you not know that if you present yourselves to anyone as obedient slaves, you are slaves of the one whom you obey, either of sin, which leads to death, or of obedience, which leads to righteousness?

How, then, do you determine whose master a given slave is serving? You look at the one to whom that slave "presents" himself. For this reason, Paul uses the word "present" several times in this chapter.

> Do not *present* your members to sin as instruments for unrighteousness, but *present* yourselves to God as those who have been brought from death to life, and your members to God as instruments for righteousness (Rom. 6:13, emphasis added)

> For just as you once *presented* your members as slaves to impurity and to lawlessness leading to more lawlessness, so now *present* your members as slaves to righteousness leading to sanctification. (Rom. 6:19, emphasis added)

In these verses, Paul speaks of two aspects of how we present ourselves to our master. On the one hand, we are not to present ourselves to our former master for service. Paul recognizes that the attractions of our former master continue to plague the believer. We must therefore resolve not to present ourselves or any part of ourselves to sin. We must carry out that resolution in practical action by saying no to sin. Paul wants us to remember that when we formerly said yes to sin because we were slaves to sin, the result was only "more lawlessness." Sin has an insatiable appetite, and we must starve it.

Paul's counsel is not purely negative. There is a crucial and corresponding positive command. We are not only to refrain from doing something, but we are to put something else in its place. Paul would have us replace the service of sin with another kind of service. We are to submit ourselves and every part of ourselves to God. We will please our new Master by pursuing and doing what is pleasing to Him, namely, righteousness. The blessed fruit of this pattern of life is sanctification, that is, increasing conformity to God's holy character.

Although Paul will spell out the shape and specifics of this righteousness later in this letter, already in this chapter he helps us to see two crucial things about this pattern of service to God: "Thanks be to God, that you . . . have become obedient from the heart to the standard of teaching to which you were committed" (Rom. 6:17). First, this service proceeds "from the heart." It is not merely external, nor does it consist simply of conformity to a certain set of behaviors. God also cares about our desires, motives, and affections. Our inner and outer lives are both encompassed under the service that God requires of us. Second, this service embraces "the standard of teaching to which [we] were committed." This "standard of teaching" is, of course, Christ's teaching by His Apostles. That is to say, our standard is the written Word of God, the Bible.[9] We are "committed" without reservation

---

9   This standard includes not only the New Testament but also the Old Testament. Christ and His Apostles not only affirmed the plenary inspiration and the inerrancy of the Old Testament, but also

or qualification to that "standard." In summary, our service or submission reaches into the depths of our being ("heart") and extends to the whole of our lives—as far as God's Word goes.

## Justification and Sanctification

We may close our observations on Romans 6 by stressing two related points that have surfaced throughout our reflections. First, justification and sanctification must be properly related to each other. They must be distinguished. We must never confuse or collapse these two graces into one another. Our justification is in no way grounded upon our sanctification. But neither may we separate justification and sanctification. Sanctification is not an optional extra in the Christian life. No Christian may claim to have been justified if he is not pursuing the life of sanctification.

Second, one way in which Paul helps us relate justification and sanctification is by placing both graces in the context of the believer's union with Christ. To be sure, justification and sanctification are two different graces. Justification is a legal act that takes place in God's courtroom. Sanctification is a renovative work that entails the transformation of our whole lives—our minds, will, affections, and behavior. Justification is perfect, unchanging, and instantaneous. Sanctification is imperfect, ongoing, and progressive. Justification concerns righteousness *imputed*; sanctification concerns righteousness *infused*. Maintaining these distinctions is crucial to a right understanding of Paul's gospel.

For all these differences, justification and sanctification have this in common: both of these benefits are ours in saving union with Christ. That is to say, all the resources that we need for the pardon of sin and for the accepting and accounting of our persons righteous in God's sight are in Christ, and all the resources that we need to be brought out from sin's dominion and to make progress against the sin that remains in us are in Christ. Paul's point is simple—never look outside of Jesus Christ in order to deal with sin and live acceptably to God. Everything we need for these matters of eternal consequence is bound up in the Savior. And that is good news for sinners.

---

included the Old Testament as part of that rule of faith and practice given to the Christian church. For Paul's fullest statement of this truth, see 2 Timothy 3:16–17.

Chapter 9

---

# PAUL'S GOSPEL—
# SANCTIFICATION (II)

In the last chapter, we observed the Apostle Paul addressing an indispensable part of the Christian gospel that he calls "sanctification" (Rom. 6:19). At the moment that we are savingly united to Christ in His death and resurrection, we are delivered from the dominion of sin and brought under the lordship of Christ. No longer enslaved to sin, impurity, and lawlessness, we now serve God and righteousness.

In view of this new relationship with both sin and righteousness, we are commanded to submit ourselves to the lordship of Christ, living unto Him by the power of His death and resurrection. In our thoughts and lives, we say no to sin and yes to righteousness. In this way, we make gradual but palpable progress against the sin that remains in our lives.

Paul knows that the Christian life is not a steady succession of unbroken victories. Neither will any of us arrive at sinless perfection in this life. It is for this reason that Romans 7 follows hard on the heels of Romans 6. Romans 7 helps us understand that the life of Romans 6 involves struggle, conflict, and even setbacks. In this regard, Romans 7 is neither unique nor unusual in Paul's teaching. From his earlier (Gal. 5:17–18) to his later (Eph. 6:13–18) correspondence, Paul impresses upon the church the fact that the Christian life is a battle that requires commitment, energy, and resources. Paul, of course, was willing to practice what he preached. He told the Corinthians, "I discipline my body and keep it under control" (1 Cor. 9:27).

Paul was not detached from this battle but placed himself in the trenches with all his fellow Christians. Nowhere is this fact on more vivid display than in Romans 7. As we will see, this chapter is one of the most grippingly autobiographical portions of all of Paul's letters.[1]

Romans 7 is not Paul's last word or only word on sanctification in Romans, but it is a needed word. In this chapter, we will look at what Paul has to say in Romans 7 about the struggle of Christian living in two related lights. First, we will see the struggle in light of the law of God. Second, we will see the struggle in light of the sin that remains in the believer.

## The Law and the Christian

If we were to say, "Romans 7 is about our sin," that would fail to capture fully what Paul is trying to accomplish in this section of Romans. It is more accurate to say that Romans 7 is an apologetic for the law. Paul must make this defense because of the tragic reality of sin in the lives of human beings.

In this regard, Romans 7 clarifies some of Paul's statements about the law in chapter 6. In Romans 6:14, he told believers, "You are not under law but under grace." In Romans 7:6 (which is technically the conclusion of Paul's argument begun at Rom. 6:1), he says of believers that "now we are released from the law, having died to that which held us captive." Such statements raise the question, is the law sin? In answer, Paul immediately replies, "By no means!" (Rom. 7:7).

In Romans 7:7–25, Paul offers a defense or vindication of the law. He does so, we will see, in two respects. First, he vindicates the law from the standpoint of his experience as an unbeliever (vv. 7–13). Second, he vindicates the law from the standpoint of his experience as a believer (vv. 14–25).

In Romans 7:7–13, Paul speaks of himself in the past tense. He is reflecting on his life in unbelief and sin. He is giving us an autobiographical account of what he earlier called "living in the flesh" (v. 5). In these verses,

---

1  Over the last century, some scholars have challenged the understanding of Romans 7 as an autobiographical chapter. The first-person pronoun ("I") is said not to refer to Paul personally or individually. Some take it as a rhetorical way for Paul to talk about the experience of Israel under the Mosaic law. The problem with that approach is that, throughout his letters, Paul typically uses the first-person singular personal pronoun ("I") of himself. Absent some clear indication in Romans 7 to the contrary, this pattern obliges us to take these pronouns to refer to the Apostle Paul as an individual.

Paul is asking and answering the question, how does the law work in such a person's life? Reflecting on his own experience, Paul answers that question in at least four ways. First, the law informed him what sin is: "If it had not been for the law, I would not have known sin" (v. 7). The example that Paul provides is coveting (vv. 7–8). God's law defines sin, telling us what sin is. Second, when reigning sin encounters the law, the result is more sin: "But sin, seizing an opportunity through the commandment, produced in me all kinds of covetousness" (v. 8). There is a kind of dormancy to sin ("apart from the law, sin lies dead"; v. 8).[2] When the law breaks into a person's experience, however, sin rises to life. Paul is clear—it is not the law but *sin* that "produced in me all kinds of covetousness." The fault never lies with God's law. It always lies with us.

The third way that Paul speaks of the law's work in a unbeliever's life concerns the result when sin meets the law. When reigning sin encounters the law and that sin produces more sin, the ultimate result is death: "For sin, seizing an opportunity through the commandment, deceived me *and through it killed me*" (Rom. 7:11, emphasis added). Sin is deceptive. It promises life and fulfillment, but it always delivers death. The law, Paul reminds us, offers life for obedience but threatens death for disobedience (v. 10). In this way, "Sin [is] shown to be sin" (v. 13). The law shows sin in all its ugly colors. It strips sin of its deceits. It declares that death is truly the wages of sin.

Fourth, as Paul brings this section of his argument to a close, Paul insists that "the law is holy, and the commandment is holy and righteous and good" (Rom. 7:12). Paul speaks of the law in terms that reflect the divine character. The law in every way reflects its divine Author. The blame, then, for sin and death falls squarely upon the sinner himself. Blame for these things cannot be shifted to God's law.

---

2   When Paul says in Romans 7:9, "I was once alive apart from the law, but when the commandment came, sin came alive and I died," he is not saying that he was genuinely spiritually alive apart from the law. He is speaking from the vantage point of self-perception. Paul is saying that before the law broke into his experience, he *thought* that he was spiritually alive. Once the law did its work, however, Paul "died," that is, he came to the realization that he was dead in his trespasses and sins. Paul, we have seen, was raised in an observant Jewish home and received a thorough Pharisaical education. It is hard to conceive of a time in his life when he was not intellectually aware of God's law. Paul must be referring in these verses to a moment in his experience when the law began to work upon his conscience and to occasion a profound sense of sinfulness. At some point in the Apostle's experience, the law that had been the lifelong subject of Paul's study and interest began to work with power on his soul.

In Romans 7:14–25, Paul proceeds to vindicate the law from the vantage point of his experience as a believer. This understanding of these verses has been a matter of some debate in the church. Many scholars and theologians (even a few Reformed scholars and theologians) have argued that Paul is not talking about the experience of the believer in this section. What are the reasons, then, for saying that Paul is speaking here about his own Christian life and, correspondingly, the Christian lives of his readers? We may point to three.

First, whereas Paul consistently used the past tense in Romans 7:7–13, he now consistently uses the present tense in 7:14–25. He proceeds from talking about who he *was* to talking about who he *is*. The change in verb tense is not accidental, and its best explanation is that Paul is now concerned to speak about his present Christian experience.

Second, Paul speaks in Romans 7:22 of his "inner man" (author's translation; ESV "inner being"). He uses this phrase in only two other places in his letters—2 Corinthians 4:16 and Ephesians 3:16. In both of these latter passages, Paul is speaking of the believer. It is therefore likely that the same phrase in Romans 7:22 refers to a believer, since Paul nowhere explicitly speaks of unbelievers as having an "inner man."

Third, Paul's posture toward the law in these verses requires us to understand him as speaking of a Christian person. Paul "agree[s] with the law, that it is good" (Rom. 7:16). He "delight[s] in the law of God, in [his] inner being" (v. 22). He "serve[s] the law of God with [his] mind" (v. 25). It is hard to imagine the Apostle Paul saying such things of an unbeliever. In the next chapter, Paul will say of the unbeliever, "The mind that is set on the flesh is hostile to God, for it does not submit to God's law; indeed, it cannot" (Rom. 8:7). How can one who does not and cannot submit to God's law at the same time agree with, delight in, and serve that law?

The experience in view in these verses, then, is that of the Christian believer. Paul tells us that the law of God continues to play the role of exposing sin in the believer's life: "Now if I do not do what I want, I agree with the law, that it is good" (Rom. 7:16). Paul acknowledges, furthermore, that "the law is spiritual" (v. 14). When Paul says that the law is "spiritual," he identifies it thoroughly with the Holy Spirit. The law is the written record of what is pleasing to the Spirit and what the Spirit wants the Christian to do.[3] In this context, the Spirituality of the law confirms that for the believer as well as for the unbeliever, blame never rests upon the law. Blame always lies with us so far as we are associated with sin (v. 14).

## The Christian's Ongoing Struggle

Paul's reflections on the law and the believer lead us to the second dimension of the Christian's struggle that Paul portrays in Romans 7. Why is it that the believer does not perfectly execute his desire to obey God's law? Why is it that the believer not only finds in himself contrary inclinations to that law but also acts on those inclinations in violation of God's law?

The answer, Paul says, is indwelling sin. Paul offers us a description of the Christian life from the vantage point of the ebb and flow of the sin that remains in each believer. He shows us four important things that we need to know about indwelling sin if we are to make progress in the Christian life.

First, while the landscape of Romans 7 is bleak, Paul has not forgotten what he said in chapter 6. There, Paul argued that in Christ, sin has been dethroned for every believer. The believer gladly and willingly submits himself to the lordship of Christ. This reality is evident throughout Romans 7:14–25 as Paul speaks of his own experience. At the core of his being, at the deepest level of who Paul is, Paul aligns himself with God's law: "I do not do what I want" (v. 15); "I agree with the law, that it is good" (v. 16); "I have the desire to do what is right" (v. 18); "When I want to do right" (v. 21); "I delight in the law of God, in my inner being" (v. 22); "I myself serve the law of God with my mind" (v. 25). No small part of Paul's grief for the sin that remains in his life is that his sin is contrary to his most fundamental desires, inclinations, and resolutions. In that sense, Paul does not want to be where he finds himself.

Second, there are in Paul remnants of the "old man" (see Rom. 6:6). That is to say, the old Adamic ways of thinking, choosing, and behaving are still present in Paul. While sin no longer reigns, it does remain. In Romans 7:18, Paul says of himself, "I know that nothing good dwells in me, that is, in my flesh. For I have the desire to do what is right, but not the ability to

---

3 It is for this reason that Paul directs the believer to the moral core of God's law, that is, the Decalogue, as the divinely appointed norm for Christian living (Rom. 13:8–10; Eph. 6:1–2).

carry it out." As the Apostle examines himself, he sees his own sin. His sin prevents him from bringing his deepest and most cherished desires to fruition. He speaks of this conflict more than once in this section: "I find it to be a law that when I want to do right, evil lies close at hand" (Rom. 7:21); "I see in my members another law" (Rom. 7:23).

Paul's way of speaking raises a question. He places his commitment to God in his "mind" (Rom. 7:23), even as he finds sin in his "members" (v. 23) or his "body" (v. 24) or his "flesh" (vv. 18, 25). Is Paul compartmentalizing himself? Is he saying that he is engaged in a struggle between his (good) mind and his (wicked) body?

He is saying no such thing. For one thing, Paul throughout this passage locates sin in himself, that is, his whole person: "Sin . . . dwells within me" (Rom. 7:17). Throughout this chapter, it is *Paul* who sins against God, not some part of Paul for which the "real" Paul is not responsible: "I do not understand my own actions . . . I do what I do not want . . . I do not do the good I want, but the evil I do not want is what I keep on doing" (vv. 15–16, 19).

Why, then, does Paul speak as he does of his mind, members, body, and flesh? These terms are not attempts to dichotomize the human person. They are, rather, different perspectives on the whole human being. For Paul, the "mind" is the center or core of one's person—that from which one's whole person finds its perspective and direction. The whole person in the expression of sin is depicted in terminology such as "members," "body," or "flesh." After all, human beings bring sin to expression in their eyes, hands, lips, feet, and so on. What Paul is saying in Romans 7:14–25 is twofold. First, Paul's most ultimate and sincerest commitments lie with Christ and His lordship ("mind"). Second, despite Paul's best intentions and efforts, indwelling sin persistently and repeatedly comes to expression in his person ("members," "body," "flesh"). Even so, Paul does not excuse himself or lay blame anywhere other than upon himself. Paul is grieved because *he* is the one who commits sin.[4]

The third thing Paul tells us about indwelling sin in the believer has to do with its extent and influence. The Apostle uses striking language to

---

4 Paul's statement in Romans 7:20 ("Now if I do what I do not want, it is no longer I who do it, but sin that dwells within me") is not backhanded extenuation or self-exoneration. It is, rather, Paul declaring that, at the core of his person, he does not identify with the sin that nevertheless adheres to and remains in his person.

capture the reach, tenacity, and power of indwelling sin. In Romans 7:14, he says that he is "of the flesh, sold under sin." In verse 23, he states, "I see in my members another law waging war against the law of my mind and making me captive to the law of sin that dwells in my members." In light of these expressions and in light of what Paul said in chapter 6, many have concluded that Paul is not speaking here of Christian experience. But if Paul is speaking of himself as a Christian, how are we to understand these expressions?

When Paul says he is "of the flesh" (Rom. 7:14) he does not say that he is "in the flesh." This difference of preposition may seem slight, but it is all important.[5] Paul does not say here that he is under the dominion of sin. "Of the flesh" means that remaining sin has manifested itself in Paul's life, to his great grief and regret. Furthermore, when Paul speaks of himself as "sold under sin" (Rom. 7:14) and "captive to the law of sin that dwells in my members" (Rom. 7:23), he is not saying that he is under the unbroken reign of sin. He is, however, giving expression to the strength, deception, and reach of remaining sin in his Christian life. The Christian life is a protracted war against sin. As in any war, there are multiple engagements with the enemy. Even when ultimate victory is assured to an army that is making progress against the enemy, individual battles may nevertheless be lost.[6] There are times in Christian warfare, Paul says, that it will seem as if the enemy has the upper hand and may, in fact, have momentary ascendancy. The struggle with sin is not to be taken casually or cavalierly. It involves serious engagement and even setbacks.

Fourth, in Paul's description of his battle with indwelling sin, we see that while Paul struggles deeply and mightily against the sin that remains in him, he does not despair. As important as it is to chart the struggles of Romans 7:14–25, it is equally important to pause over its triumphant (but not triumphalist) conclusion: "Wretched man that I am! Who will deliver me from this body of death? Thanks be to God through Jesus Christ our

---

5 A single Greek word underlies what the ESV renders "of the flesh." This Greek word is an adjective and could be rendered less elegantly as "fleshlike" or "fleshly."

6 The mid-twentieth-century New Testament scholar Oscar Cullmann used the illustration of the Allied Forces between D-Day and V-E Day at the end of World War II. D-Day ensured an Allied victory over Nazi Germany. Many grueling battles, however, lay between the invasion of Normandy and Germany's surrender. The Allies did not win all of these battles even though they were progressing toward what was then expected to be a victorious outcome.

Lord! So then, I myself serve the law of God with my mind, but with my flesh I serve the law of sin" (Rom. 7:24–25). To the degree that Paul finds himself associated with sin, he declares himself "wretched." In that respect, his body, so far as it is indwelt by sin, he calls "this body of death." And yet, that bleak self-assessment prompts Paul to look outside himself for help. We may paraphrase his question, "Who will deliver me from myself?" There is a deliverer, namely, Jesus Christ our Lord. Because Jesus is the believer's deliverer, Paul does not lapse into utter despair. His hope of deliverance lies entirely outside himself. Paul therefore has the confidence and assurance that he needs to continue on in this struggle. He knows that he does not labor in vain.

The opening verse of Romans 8 provides an important insight into one reason why Paul draws such confidence from Christ, "There is therefore now no condemnation for those who are in Christ Jesus" (Rom. 8:1). As Paul wars against the sin that remains—sin that he detests and hates and with which he refuses to identify himself at the core of his person—he reminds himself that he is a justified person. Paul is not freed from condemnation because of his sincerity or progress in the struggle against sin. He is freed from condemnation because of the gift of Christ's righteousness imputed to him and received through faith alone (Rom. 5:12–21). Because Paul has irreversibly entered into a justified state, he knows that he will never fall back into the condemnation that his sins deserve. Paul's sincerity in the struggle—his fundamental alignment with God and his law and his corresponding breach with sin—in no way justifies him. It does, however, evidence to him that he belongs to the Christ in whom alone he is justified.

## Lessons for Today

What lessons does Paul's teaching in Romans 7 have for Christians today? First, Paul reminds us that the Christian life involves struggle and conflict. Every true Christian discovers at some point the power and reach of indwelling sin. The fact that we have made the decisive break with sin and have begun to experience resurrection life in Christ only seems to accentuate the problem. The sudden surprises that indwelling sin can make, the things that we may find ourselves saying and doing—things of which we had thought ourselves incapable or against which we had resolved, prayed, and labored—may well conspire to tempt us to doubt and despair.

Paul helps us see that this kind of struggle is something that we should expect in the Christian life. The unbeliever is incapable of experiencing this particular struggle. He has no true love for God and does not share the Christian's delight in and commitment to the law of God. When the believer finds himself grieved over the presence and power of remaining sin and his inability to serve God the way that he wants, the believer should recognize this grief as evidence of the grace of Christ in his life. When the believer is sincerely committed to Christ's lordship and, in spite of himself, finds himself engaged in sin and even, as it were, in the vice grip of sin, it is then that he may and ought to redouble his efforts to fight sin with confidence. How can he do so? He must first remind himself that he belongs to Christ, that there is no condemnation for those who are in Christ Jesus, and that Christ has won for him the resources he needs to wage well the war against sin.

The abiding significance of the saving work of Christ leads to a second lesson for us regarding our remaining sin. The Christian life is one of unceasing dependence upon Christ. In living the Christian life and especially in waging war against sin, we are tempted to slacken our commitment both to combat sin and to pursue holiness. We are also tempted to grow complacent and think that we simply have it in ourselves to combat sin and to obey God, neglecting Christ and losing sight of our complete dependence upon Him. Sometimes we are even tempted to think that God has forgiven us or accepts us because of how well we think that we have lived the Christian life. In each of these situations, we are forgetting or neglecting the vital truths about the saving work of Christ that Paul has labored to explain in Romans.

Sometimes it is the renewed and surprising expression or sense of indwelling sin that prompts us to go back to first things. It is at such a point in our Christian experience that Paul's closing words in Romans 7 should come home. A right sense of indwelling sin should lead us to disavow complacency or unwholesome self-dependence. It should also send us afresh into the arms of our only deliverer, Christ. And when that happens, we should say, with the Apostle Paul, "Thanks be to God through Jesus Christ our Lord!" (Rom. 7:25).

# Chapter 10

---

# PAUL'S GOSPEL—
# SANCTIFICATION (III)

In the previous two chapters, we contemplated what Paul's gospel has to say about growth and change in the Christian life. Specifically, we have surveyed that part of his gospel that the Apostle terms "sanctification" (Rom. 6:19). Foundational to the project of Christian renovation is the believer's self-awareness that he is savingly united to Christ in His death and resurrection. In Christ, we have been transferred from bondage to sin and have been brought into the realm of resurrection life. We now gladly live under the dominion of Jesus Christ. Paul has reminded us in Romans 7 that sin continues to indwell the believer (Rom. 7:17). The Christian therefore engages in a lifelong struggle or conflict with sin. While assured that sin will not get the final word (Rom. 7:24–8:1), the believer experiences many ups and downs in his battle with sin.

Paul has yet in Romans to treat in depth one of the most crucial aspects of our sanctification: the sanctifying ministry of the Holy Spirit in the lives of God's people. To be sure, in the first seven chapters of Romans, Paul has spoken of the person and work of the Spirit. God by the Spirit raised Jesus from the dead, ushering Him, in His humanity, into the life of the age to come (Rom. 1:4). The Spirit is the one who circumcises the heart (Rom. 2:29). The Spirit "has been given" to believers and ensures that "God's love [is] poured into our hearts" (Rom. 5:5). Fittingly, believers "serve in the new way of the Spirit," looking to the law that the Spirit has authored and given to us as the standard for living that is pleasing to God (Rom. 7:6, 14).

It is in Romans 8, however, that Paul's exposition of the ministry of the Spirit reaches its crescendo. What is it that Paul wants us to know about the ministry of the Spirit in our Christian lives? We may look at Paul's reflections on the Spirit's work along two lines. First, the Spirit indwells each believer. Second, the Spirit is the Spirit of adoption as sons.

## The Indwelling Spirit

Paul wants us to see that the Spirit indwells each believer. The Spirit's indwelling is not a privilege that is bestowed on only a handful of Christians. Every Christian is indwelt by the Spirit. For this reason, Paul says that unless one is indwelt by the Spirit, he is not a true Christian: "You . . . are not in the flesh but in the Spirit, if in fact the Spirit of God dwells in you. Anyone who does not have the Spirit of Christ does not belong to him" (Rom. 8:9). Paul knows only two conditions of human beings. We are either "in the flesh" (in Adam) or "in the Spirit" (in Christ). The Christian is necessarily "in the Spirit." If this is not the case, Paul insists, then that person "does not belong to [Christ]."

This claim is an extraordinary one. To understand and appreciate it, we need to give some thought to who the Spirit is and to the meaning of His indwelling presence in the life of the Christian.

Who is the Spirit? Paul elsewhere shows us that he understands the Spirit to be God.[1] The Spirit is not, furthermore, an emanation of God or a way of speaking of one of the attributes or activities of God.[2] He is one of the three persons of the Godhead. One God exists eternally in three persons: Father, Son, and Holy Spirit. The Spirit is a divine person, the equal of God the Father and God the Son.

As he does in many places in his letters, Paul identifies the Holy Spirit in Romans 8:9–11 as the One by whom God raised Jesus from the dead. Paul,

---

1 Paul offers no formal argument for the deity of the Spirit. He shows us that he understands the Spirit to be God when he sets the Spirit as an equal alongside God the Father and God the Son (1 Cor. 12:3–6; 2 Cor. 13:14; Eph. 4:4–6).

2 See the personal attributes ascribed to the Spirit in 1 Corinthians 12:11, where it is the Spirit "who apportions to each one individually as he wills," and in Ephesians 4:30, where Paul cautions us not to "grieve the Holy Spirit of God."

in fact, has introduced us to God the Holy Spirit in the opening verses of Romans along just these lines: "[His Son, who] was declared to be the Son of God in power according to the Spirit of holiness by his resurrection from the dead" (Rom. 1:4). Jesus' dead humanity was brought to life by the Spirit.

But Paul is not saying that Jesus was merely resuscitated. Jesus was ushered into a new phase of His messianic Sonship—the resurrection declared Him to be the "Son of God in power." This new phase of Sonship, then, was characterized by "power," even as in the days of His humiliation, His Sonship had been marked by weakness.

Paul attributes this "power" to the ministry of the Spirit in raising the second Adam from the dead.[3] The Spirit powerfully raised and transformed the humanity of Jesus Christ, ushering Jesus into a realm—the age to come—that is defined by the presence and activity of the Spirit.[4] The resurrected Jesus and the Spirit by whom God raised Jesus from the dead now work in tandem in order to bring into the lives of God's people those resources of the age to come that Christ secured by His obedience, death, and resurrection.[5]

All the benefits and blessings that the believer receives are sourced *in* Christ, are supplied *by* Christ, and are conveyed to us *by the ministry* of the Holy Spirit. It is for this reason that Paul can speak comprehensively of the redemptive blessings that belong to the Christian as "spiritual": "Blessed be the God and Father of our Lord Jesus Christ, who has blessed us in Christ with every spiritual blessing in the heavenly places" (Eph. 1:3).[6]

---

3  Paul consistently speaks of Jesus as having been raised from the dead. Resurrection, we may say, is something that was done to Him. What, then, are we to make of Jesus' words in John's gospel that Jesus raised Himself by His own divine power (see John 10:17–18)? There is neither disagreement nor contradiction between Paul and John. John references Jesus' resurrection in light of Jesus' deity. Without denying Jesus' divine agency in raising Himself from the dead, Paul speaks of the resurrection of Jesus in light of Jesus' humanity, which was entirely passive in its resurrection from the dead. Paul does so in order to help us see the similarities between Jesus' experience of resurrection as the second Adam and our own experience of resurrection as those who are in Christ, the second Adam.

4  Paul elsewhere reflects on this momentous transformation in 1 Corinthians 15, especially verses 44–49.

5  It is in light of this functional identity that Paul elsewhere can say that at the resurrection, Jesus "became life-giving Spirit" (1 Cor. 15:45, author's translation) so that now "the Lord is the Spirit" (2 Cor. 3:17).

6  Notice once again the Trinitarian shape of this verse. The Father blesses us in Christ by the Spirit.

This general framework for the person and ministry of the Spirit in Paul's teaching helps us appreciate what he tells us about the Spirit in Romans 8. Paul identifies the Spirit in a variety of ways in verses 9–11. He is the "Spirit" (vv. 9–10), the "Spirit of God" (v. 9; see v. 11, "his Spirit"), the "Spirit of Christ" (v. 9), and "the Spirit of him who raised Jesus from the dead" (v. 11). Here, Paul reminds us of the importance of understanding the Spirit's role in raising Jesus from the dead. That is to say, we are to think of the Spirit as the giver of resurrection life. We are also to think of the Spirit in relation to Christ: He is "the Spirit of Christ." The Spirit is not a free agent who works independently of Christ. The Spirit and Christ work together.

Paul underscores this point in striking fashion. Who is the One whom Paul says indwells the believer? In Romans 8:9, it is "the Spirit of God," and in verse 11, "the Spirit of him who raised Jesus from the dead" or "his Spirit." But in verse 10, it is "Christ." So closely do the Spirit and Christ work together in the lives of God's people that Paul can interchange them when speaking of who it is who indwells us. Paul is, of course, not confusing or collapsing the persons of the Spirit and of Christ into one another. He is saying, rather, that while personally distinct, they are one in their mission of the application of redemption. For this reason, Paul can also put the point negatively: "Anyone who does not have the Spirit of Christ does not belong to him" (v. 9). No one belongs to Jesus Christ unless the Spirit has taken up residence in that person's life. The Spirit's indwelling is not an option or an extra in the Christian life. It is a basic and indispensable part of truly belonging to Jesus Christ. The reason is both simple and clear: because of the close association between the risen Jesus and the Spirit, no believer can have one without the other.

Now that we have seen that the Spirit's indwelling is essential to the Christian life, we may ask what the abiding presence of the Spirit means for our Christian lives. In Romans 8, Paul speaks of the Spirit's ministry in both present and future terms.

What does it mean for our present that the Spirit indwells us? In the first place, it means, as we have seen, that He has taken up residence in our lives. He has made us His home. Elsewhere, Paul explains this reality in terms of the Old Testament tabernacle and temple. Just as God made His home in the temple of old, so now He makes His home in that which the temple anticipated—the "temple" that is our body (1 Cor. 6:19; see 3:16).[7] But whereas God withdrew from the old covenant temple in judgment on His people, He pledges to abide in His people all the way until the resurrection of their bodies (Rom. 8:11).

This indwelling is not only permanent but also epochal or aeonic. That is to say, the Spirit's indwelling is evidence that we have been brought from one order ("in the flesh") to another order ("in the Spirit"). "You, however, are not in the flesh but in the Spirit, if in fact the Spirit of God dwells in you" (Rom. 8:9). Recall that "flesh" and "Spirit" describe two antithetical orders or eons—this present age, characterized by weakness, sin, corruption, and death; and the age to come, characterized by power, life, blessing, and glory. When the Spirit united us to Christ, Paul is saying, we were transferred from one realm ("flesh") to the other ("Spirit"). We no longer live under the dominion of and in bondage to the flesh. We now live under the dominion of the Spirit. What is pleasing to the Spirit now directs and governs us.

In Romans 8, Paul characterizes this new existence with the word "life." "But if Christ is in you, although the body is dead because of sin, the Spirit is life because of righteousness" (Rom. 8:10). In other words, we may paraphrase Paul, "In you is sin and death, but the Spirit brings life." How can the Spirit bring the "life" of the age to come to those who are dead because of sin? The answer is on the basis of "righteousness," namely, the righteousness of Christ, imputed to us and received through faith alone (see Rom. 8:1–4).

In characterizing this new resurrection life that we receive from the Spirit because of Christ's obedience, death, and resurrection, Paul tells us in Romans 8:14 that true believers are "led by the Spirit of God" (see Gal. 5:18). By "leading," Paul does not have in mind momentary impulses or urges, the way that people sometimes misguidedly speak of the Spirit's leading. He has in mind, rather, the Spirit's giving direction and guidance to the whole of our lives. Our thinking, choices, behavior—indeed, our very dispositions—have been radically changed. We now live to say yes to the Spirit and no to the flesh.

Paul describes that lifestyle in broad terms in the opening verses of Romans 8. We are to "set [our] minds on the things of the Spirit" and not

---

7 And we, of course, are called God's temple because we have been incorporated into Christ (see Eph. 2:11–22).

"on the things of the flesh" (Rom. 8:5). Just as Paul has argued in Romans 6, the indispensable first step of sanctification is orienting our thinking to what God has revealed in His Word. Coupled with such a "mind" is a corresponding "walk" or lifestyle—"walk not according to the flesh but according to the Spirit" (Rom. 8:4). We are not to "live according to the flesh" but to "live according to the Spirit" (Rom. 8:5).

What does such a lifestyle look like in practice? When we were in the flesh, we were "hostile to God" and did "not submit to God's law" (Rom. 8:7). Now that we are God's friends, reconciled to Him in Christ, we delight in and commit ourselves to keeping the law of God. Furthermore, "by the Spirit [we] put to death the deeds of the body" (Rom. 8:13). We kill or put to death or "mortify" our sin. That is to say, we aim at nothing less than eradicating sin from our lives wherever it may be found. We fight it, weaken it, starve it, deprive it of life. We do so, Paul stresses, "by the Spirit"—in the strength and by the means that the Spirit supplies. Life in the Spirit, then, carries both a negative and a positive aspect. We must say no to sin (by killing it) and we must say yes to the Spirit (by obeying the law that is "spiritual"; Rom. 7:14).

Paul is clear that this lifestyle is not optional for the Christian. The sole alternative to life in the Spirit is life in the flesh (Rom. 8:5). A settled commitment to living in the flesh results only in "death" (Rom. 8:6, 13). Correlatively, the presence of a lifestyle "in the flesh" is evidence that the Spirit does not indwell such a person. And if the Spirit does not indwell such a person, then he does not belong to Christ.

On the other hand, Paul has helped us in these verses to answer the question, how can one know that he is a true Christian? Paul invites us to look in our lives for evidence of the Spirit's working. Does our lifestyle show us and others that the Spirit has taken up residence in our lives? If we see the outworking of the Spirit's "mind" and "life" in our own lives, then we can know that we truly belong to Christ in the present (Rom. 8:5, 10).

What does it mean for our future that the Spirit indwells us? It means that we have the hope of nothing less than the glorious resurrection body. "If the Spirit of him who raised Jesus from the dead dwells in you, he who raised Christ Jesus from the dead will also give life to your mortal bodies through his Spirit who dwells in you" (Rom. 8:11).

It is important that we follow Paul's reasoning closely. Paul is saying that *if* the Spirit indwells us now (and we therefore experience now the "life" that He brings), *then* we may know (now) that God, by this same Spirit, will *also give life to our mortal bodies* (that is, what He did for Jesus' humanity in His bodily resurrection, the Spirit will do for our humanity in our bodily resurrection). The presence and activity of the Spirit now assures us of glorious resurrection hope in the future. If He ministers life to us now, He will minister life to us then.[8] There is no possibility that the Spirit will not finish what He has started. The Spirit will not give up on us and abandon us in the grave. He did not do that to Jesus; He will not do that to us.

## The Spirit of Adoption

The second line of teaching about God the Holy Spirit in Romans 8 concerns the Spirit as "the Spirit of adoption as sons" (Rom. 8:15). To appreciate this aspect of the Spirit's ministry in our lives, we need first to understand the Spirit's relation to Christ, the Son of God. We have seen from Romans 1:4 that Jesus' resurrection from the dead meant that Jesus was "declared to be the Son of God in power." That is to say, by the Spirit, Jesus, the last Adam, entered into a new phase of His messianic Sonship. Those who are united to Christ and indwelt by the Spirit come to share in something of that Sonship. By the Spirit's ministry, we are sons of God in and for the Son of God. What precisely does this dimension of the Spirit's work look like in our Christian experience? We may point to three realities that Paul highlights in Romans 8.

First, we now have access to the Father. We are now "sons of God" (Rom. 8:14), that is, sons of the Father. We were not born into this world as "sons of God." Formerly, in Adam, we were "sons of disobedience" and "children of wrath" (Eph. 2:2–3). The Father has brought us into His family by the redeeming work of Christ, His own Son (Gal. 4:4; Eph. 2:13, 19). In view of Christ's finished work, the Father "has sent the Spirit of his Son into our hearts" (Gal. 4:6).

As sons who belong to the family of God, we now by the Spirit "cry, 'Abba! Father!'" (Rom. 8:15). It is in Christ that we have access to the One whom we address as our heavenly Father: "In [Christ] we have boldness and

---

8  For Paul, the "life" that we now experience in Christ, by the Spirit, is of a piece with the fullness of "life" that we will consummately experience at our bodily resurrection.

access with confidence through our faith in him" (Eph. 3:12). This access gives us the privilege of coming to God as our Father in prayer. We call upon God in the same terms that Jesus did when He was on earth. Just as Jesus called upon God as "Abba, Father" in His hour of distress in Gethsemane, so we may call upon God as our Father in our deep distress (Mark 14:36). The Spirit ensures that in such times, we will cry out to our Father and find help in our hour of need. It is on just such occasions that "the Spirit himself bears witness with our spirit that we are children of God" (Rom. 8:16).

Second, our adoption as children of the Father in Christ by the Spirit means that we are heirs with Christ. Notice how Paul infers the privilege of inheritance from our adoption: "If children, then heirs—heirs of God and fellow heirs with Christ, provided we suffer with him in order that we may also be glorified with him" (Rom. 8:17; see Gal. 4:7). Paul lived in a world where the oldest son was typically designated his father's heir. Jesus Christ, the Son of God, has entered into His inheritance upon His exaltation. Christ withholds nothing of this inheritance from His people. United to Christ, each believer shares in the fullness of that inheritance—so much so that we are counted "heirs of God and fellow heirs with Christ." How do we know that we will fully enter into the blessing, life, and glory that Jesus Christ possesses presently? We may be certain of these things because we are sons of God and therefore heirs of God and fellow-heirs with the Son of God. And because it is the Spirit's delight to testify to our spirits "that we are children of God" (Rom. 8:16), we are therefore assured of ongoing reminders of our standing as heirs in Christ.

Third, Paul ties our adoption by the Spirit to our ongoing conformity after the image of Jesus Christ. At the end of Romans 8:17, Paul describes the Christian life in this way: we *suffer* with Christ in order that we may be *glorified* with Christ. Paul's statement reminds us that Christ's own earthly life and ministry followed this exact pattern. Jesus first suffered and then entered into glory (see Phil. 2:6–11; 2 Cor. 13:4). In union and communion with Christ, by the power of the Spirit, Paul continues, our Christian lives reflect this pattern. While we have had hints and tastes of glory in our Christian lives (2 Cor. 3:18), the fullness of that glory awaits us. For the present, believers are called to suffer, and their union and communion with Jesus Christ gives that suffering profound meaning and significance (see 2 Cor. 4:7–18). What Paul is saying in Romans 8:17 is that our experience of sonship involves not only awaiting the inheritance but also being conformed to the life pattern of Jesus Christ. This progressive fashioning after the likeness of Christ is the concern of the Spirit.

Paul reflects further on this reality later in Romans 8. In one of the most well-known statements of Paul, the Apostle tells believers, "And we know that for those who love God all things work together for good, for those who are called according to his purpose" (Rom. 8:28). This is not a promise for all people but for believers only ("for those who love God"; "for those who are called according to his purpose"). The promise is that "all things work together for good." Paul does not say that all things *are* good but that all things "work together for good." The sovereign God assures us that every detail of our lives will work *for* our good.

What is that "good"? Paul answers this question in the following verses: "For those whom he foreknew he also predestined to be conformed to the image of his Son, in order that he might be the firstborn among many brothers. And those whom he predestined he also called, and those whom he called he also justified, and those whom he justified he also glorified" (Rom. 8:29–30).

Our ultimate good is our glorification in and with Christ. We will share in glory with Christ (see Rom. 8:17). Paul here helps us understand simultaneously what that glory looks like and what that "good" is unto which God appoints and directs every circumstance of our lives: we are being "conformed to the image of his Son." The glory to which we look forward is full conformity to the second Adam. Every detail of our lives is ordained so that we will be more and more conformed after the image of Christ. The Spirit's commitment to our sonship is, in effect, a commitment to the glory of Christ, who is "the firstborn among many brothers." The Spirit is at work in our lives to make us more and more Christlike. Presently we have the "firstfruits of the Spirit," but we "wait eagerly for adoption as sons, the redemption of our bodies" (Rom. 8:23). This final installment in the experience of our adoption will be the Spirit's capstone on His own glorious endeavor—that a people, redeemed and brought into God's family as sons, would be consummately conformed to Jesus Christ, the "firstborn among many brothers."

## Lessons for Today

What lessons does Paul's glorious and expansive teaching about the ministry of the Spirit in Romans 8 have for the church today? Though there are many, we will mention only two here. First, we live in a day when the Spirit and His work are the subject of much interest and discussion in the Christian church. Sadly, however, the Spirit and His work have become the occasion of much controversy and division within the church as well. Paul gives us the clarity that we need to appreciate and value the Spirit's ministry in the church. Central for Paul is that the Spirit is the Spirit *of Christ.* The Spirit delights to magnify and to glorify Christ. It is the Spirit's work to take what Christ has once for all accomplished for His people and to apply it in time to His people. The Spirit's purpose is to see that Christ's people are conformed after their elder brother's image. The church is frequently tempted to divorce the Spirit from Christ, to look for His special working and activity independent of Christ and of the salvation that He has won for His people. But if we are to "keep in step with the Spirit" (Gal. 5:25), we must first align ourselves with the Spirit's priorities and commitments. And that means that we also pursue Christlikeness in our own lives and promote Christlikeness in the lives of God's people around us.

Second, thoughtful study of Romans 8 yields to the Christian comfort and support in times of trouble. This chapter highlights two anchors for the Christian in the throes of trial and suffering. The first is that God is our heavenly Father. He has brought us into His family as His sons. We have full access to Him. We are His heirs in Jesus Christ. The second is that the Spirit is the Spirit of adoption as sons. He commits to minister to us in times of deep trouble (Rom. 8:15) and pledges never to leave nor to forsake us (Rom. 8:11). These are rich privileges that Paul knows we may well forget. He would not have us "fall back into fear" (Rom. 8:15) but step forward in the confidence that our sovereign Father, in and for His Son and our Savior, and by the invincible power of the Spirit of adoption as sons, is indeed working all things together for our everlasting good. It is when we understand what certainly lies in our future that we are able to face the uncertain present with Christian confidence.

# Chapter 11

# PAUL AND THE CHURCH

P aul's gospel tells us how the righteous God saves unrighteous sinners from their sins. This salvation is a complete salvation. We are released from the guilt of sin. We are brought out from the dominion of sin. One day, at the resurrection, we shall be fully delivered from the presence and influence of sin in our lives. We will then be consummately conformed after the image of our elder brother, Jesus Christ.

This good news is both personal and individual. That is to say, the offer of salvation comes to individual people and bids them repent and believe in Jesus. No one can repent and believe on their behalf. They must heed the call to repent and believe in Christ. They are culpable if they refuse Christ's overtures of mercy in the gospel.

But while the gospel has individual application, it is not individualistic. That is, believers are not left to live in isolation. The Christian life is not a solitary existence. It is a life that must be lived within a unique community. This community is one that God has created for Himself. He sustains, defends, extends, and matures it by the power of His Spirit. The moment a person becomes a Christian, he is enfolded into this body as one of its living members.[1]

---

1 To say this is not to deny that Paul understood the children of professing believers to have an acknowledged relationship with the church. Paul addresses children as members of the Ephesian church in Ephesians 6:1–3, giving them expressly Christian incentives to obey God's law. To say this is also not to affirm that being a church member necessarily means that one is thereby vitally united with Christ and a saved person. For Paul, church membership is no sure sign or guarantee

We are talking, of course, about the church. To help us understand what the church is and what it means to be part of the church, Paul uses a number of pictures from daily life. One such picture is that of the family or household: the church is "the household of God, . . . the church of the living God, a pillar and buttress of truth" (1 Tim. 3:15). Paul most frequently evokes this image when he addresses believers as "brothers." This way of speaking to and of Christians reminds us that we are all members of a spiritual family. In Christ, our elder brother, we are all brothers one with another.[2]

Paul also speaks of the church using the architectural image of a building. Specifically, he describes believers as God's temple (1 Cor. 3:16–17; 6:19; Eph. 2:21–22). We are God's temple because the Holy Spirit has taken up residence in us.[3]

The image to which Paul gives the most sustained attention is that of the human body. Paul depicts the church as an organic, living human being. In this chapter, we will first note the way that Paul speaks of the church as a body in Romans and 1 Corinthians. We will then look at how Paul describes the church as a body in two of his later letters, Ephesians and Colossians.

## The Church in Romans and 1 Corinthians

In Romans 12 and 1 Corinthians 12, Paul stresses two things about the church in relation to her identity as a body of believers—the unity that is hers and the gifts that she has received.

---

of the possession of salvation. In various ways in his letters, Paul recognizes that it is possible to hold membership in the visible church without having been truly converted (on which see Rom. 8:1–11; 2 Cor. 13:5; 2 Tim. 4:10).

2 Paul's familial language is inclusive and not exclusive of women in the church. Although Paul typically speaks of believers as "sons" of God, on one occasion he speaks of believers as "sons and daughters" in relation to their heavenly Father (2 Cor. 6:18). The masculine "sons" (and "brothers," we may infer) is therefore inclusive of all believers, male and female. Why does Paul typically address believers as "brothers" and not "brothers and sisters"? One consideration surely concerns Paul's desire to help us see our family identity in relation to our elder *brother*, Jesus Christ. Paul also wants us to understand that, as adopted sons in and for Jesus Christ, we are heirs of God (see Rom. 8:14–17). In Jewish culture, inheritances were typically left to sons in the family.

3 Paul has no discomfort conjoining more than one image of the church. Notice how Paul, in writing to the Ephesians, seamlessly moves from talking about the church as family to the church as temple: "members of the household of God, built on the foundation of the apostles and prophets, Christ Jesus himself being the cornerstone, in whom the whole structure, being joined together, grows into a holy temple in the Lord" (Eph. 2:19–21).

In discussing the church as a body, Paul first stresses the unity of the church. The church is "one body . . . we, though many, are one body in Christ" (Rom. 12:4–5). "For just as the body is one and has many members, and all the members of the body, though many, are one body, so it is with Christ" (1 Cor. 12:12). Paul does not tell the church to pursue a unity that she does not have. On the contrary, Paul tells the church that she is already in possession of a unity that is uniquely hers. The unity of which Paul speaks is a given, a reality that is already in place "in Christ" (Rom. 12:5).

It is striking that both the church in Rome and the church in Corinth appear to have had problems with unlawful divisions and factions within their respective congregations (see Rom. 14:1–15:13; 1 Cor. 1:10–4:21). The scandal of such divisions and factions is that they impede the church from expressing the unity that is presently hers in Christ. If the church is already one body in Christ, then her life together must reflect that reality. The sorts of divisions that affected the churches of Rome and Corinth were a lamentable commentary on these churches' failure to live up to the standard to which Christ had called her. The church should never tolerate, much less facilitate, such unlawful and ungodly divisions.[4]

To that end, Paul also wants to help the church understand that she, as a body, possesses gifts that Christ has given her through the Spirit. In the church at Corinth, these gifts, sadly, had become the occasion of pride and disorder. In 1 Corinthians 12, Paul helps us understand the nature, purpose, and function of gifts in the church as the body of Christ. We may summarize Paul's teaching under four headings.

First, prior to any gift in the church is the Giver of those gifts, the Holy Spirit. "For in one Spirit we were all baptized into one body—Jews or Greeks, slaves or free—and all were made to drink of one Spirit" (1 Cor. 12:13).[5] What Paul is describing in these verses applies to all Christians ("we were *all* baptized into one body"; "*all* were made to drink," emphasis added), and

---

4 This is not to say that any and all division is sinful. When a particular church renounces the authority of Scripture or essential teachings of the Bible, it thereby ceases to have any right to call itself a Christian church (on the indispensability of both these matters to the church's existence, see Gal. 1:6–10; Eph. 2:20–22; 2 Tim. 3:15–17). In such a case, members of that gathering must find and affiliate with a congregation that, in fact, stands "on the foundation of the apostles and prophets, Christ Jesus himself being the cornerstone" (Eph. 2:20).

5 I am indebted to the discussion of this verse at Richard B. Gaffin Jr., *Perspectives on Pentecost* (Phillipsburg, N.J.: P&R, 1979), 28–32.

not only to some subset of the church. He is describing what has been true of believers since we were all "baptized." By "baptized," Paul has in mind the Spirit's savingly uniting us to the risen Christ.[6] At the moment that we were united with Christ, Paul continues, we were incorporated into the one body of Christ. We were also "made to drink of one Spirit"; that is, all believers were made to share in the one Spirit and His ministry in the church. The Spirit, therefore, has united every true believer to Christ and has made the believer, incorporated into the body of Christ to partake of the Spirit's own ministry. While Paul in no way diminishes or undercuts the importance of gifts in the church, he wants believers to understand that the gifts should never overshadow their Giver, the Holy Spirit.

Second, we learn from Paul's teaching on the Spirit and His gifting that all gifts proceed from the Giver, the Holy Spirit. "There are varieties of gifts, but the same Spirit" (1 Cor. 12:4). "All these [gifted persons] are empowered by one and the same Spirit, who apportions to each one individually as he wills" (1 Cor. 12:11). "As it is, God arranged the members in the body, each one of them, as he chose" (1 Cor. 12:18). God the Spirit distributes all gifts within the church. He distributes them sovereignly, that is, according to His own will. Furthermore, the Spirit empowers those gifts, making them effective in the church. For this reason, there is no ground for boasting about the gifts that one possesses and exercises in the church. All glory goes to God the Spirit.

Third, the Spirit gives gifts for a specific purpose. "To each is given the manifestation of the Spirit for the common good" (1 Cor. 12:7). "Since you are eager for manifestations of the Spirit, strive to excel in building up the church" (1 Cor. 14:12). To understand Paul's point, we should appreciate the distinction in Paul's writings between spiritual "gifts" and the grace of sanctification. Both are supplied by the Spirit to the church, but there is a crucial difference between them. Gifts differ from the grace of sanctification in that, whereas this grace is given to sanctify a believer in Christ, gifts are given to edify the body as a whole. Put negatively, a believer's sanctification is not a function of the gifts that he possesses. As Paul argues in 1 Corinthians 13, a person may possess and exercise extraordinary gifts, but without

---

6   Recall how in Romans 6, Paul uses baptismal language in describing our union with Jesus Christ. Paul speaks this way because the sacrament of baptism is both sign and seal of union with Christ.

love, he is "nothing" (1 Cor. 13:2). One is not more or less holy because of the gifts that he possesses or lacks.

The purpose of gifts, rather, is for the building up or edification of the body as a whole. That is to say, the Spirit is pleased to assign and render effective gifts in order to mature the church. How do these gifts build up the church? One clue comes from the way in which Paul speaks of gifts at the end of 1 Corinthians 12:

> Now you are the body of Christ and individually members of it. And God has appointed in the church first apostles, second prophets, third teachers, then miracles, then gifts of healing, helping, administrating, and various kinds of tongues. Are all apostles? Are all prophets? Are all teachers? Do all work miracles? Do all possess gifts of healing? Do all speak with tongues? Do all interpret? But earnestly desire the higher gifts.
>
> And I will show you a still more excellent way. (1 Cor. 12:27–31)

Paul begins this list of gifts by mentioning three groups of people in the church—"apostles," "prophets," and "teachers." That he enumerates them ("first," "second," "third") suggests a ranking or hierarchy of gifts. What these three groups have in common is that each ministers the Word of God in the church. The "higher gifts" (v. 31) are those gifts that bring the Word of God before the church and, in this way, edify or build up the church.[7] The Spirit, then, is now pleased to edify the church in the same way that He is pleased to extend the church—by means of the preaching and teaching of the Word of God, ministered by men whom the Spirit has called to that work (see Acts 13:1–3). For all the diversity of gifts in the Christian church, Paul would have us most prize those gifts that are best adapted to growing believers in the grace and knowledge of Christ. These gifts set God's Word before His people.

Fourth, as Paul talks about the Spirit and His gifts in 1 Corinthians 12, he insists that no one person possesses all the gifts. This fact is one reason

---

7  This is not to say that all of these gifts continue in the church today. As we will see below, Paul gives us reason to think that the offices of Apostle and prophet have ceased with the passing of the Apostles and prophets of the first century.

why Paul spends so much time comparing the church to the human body in verses 12–31. In the body, every limb or member is a genuine and contributing part of the whole: "If the foot should say, 'Because I am not a hand, I do not belong to the body,' that would not make it any less a part of the body" (v. 15). Just as "weaker" members of the human body prove "indispensable," and "less honorable" members are accorded "greater honor," so also in the church (vv. 22–23). Paul goes on to say that the diversity of gifts in the church is no liability to the church. It is, on the contrary, necessary to her existence: "If all were a single member, where would the body be?" (v. 19). God has so constituted this diversity of gifts, furthermore, that every member of the body needs the others. No member may say to a different member, "I have no need of you" (v. 21). We "all suffer together" and "all rejoice together" when one member suffers or rejoices (v. 26). The divisions in Corinth and the pride that fed those divisions were corrosive of this mutuality-in-diversity.

## The Church in Ephesians and Colossians

In two of his later letters, Ephesians and Colossians, Paul returns to his comparison of the church with a human body. One striking and leading feature of Paul's reflections on what he calls "the body of Christ" (Eph. 4:12) in these letters is the emphasis that he puts on Jesus' Headship over the church. In Colossians 1:18, Paul says Jesus "is the head of the body, the church," and, in the following chapter, "the Head, from whom the whole body, nourished and knit together through its joints and ligaments, grows with a growth that is from God" (Col. 2:19). Paul stresses the same point throughout his letter to the Ephesians (Eph. 1:22; 4:15; see 4:12; 5:23).

Paul's affirmation that Christ is head over His body, the church, raises at least two questions. First, what does it mean that Christ is head of His church? Second, how does that reality help us understand the life and growth of the church?

Paul understands the meaning of Christ's Headship over His church in at least two ways. The first is in terms of Christ's authority over His church: "[The Father] put all things under his feet and gave him as head over all things to the church" (Eph. 1:22). Paul speaks here of the heavenly ascension and session of Jesus Christ. The Father has given His exalted Son dominion over nothing less than "all things." Christ is "head" over "all things" with particular reference "to the church." Jesus, then, is Lord and King of His church (see Col. 1:18). It is in that sense that He is her head.

The second meaning of Christ's Headship over the church is seen in terms of Christ's ongoing work to grow and to mature His church. Christ is, in other words, the source of the church's life, "the Head, from whom the whole body . . . grows with a growth that is from God" (Col. 2:19). Jesus not only rules over His body, the church, but He also sees to it that she grows with a growth that He uniquely supplies her.

How, then, does the fact that Christ is head over His church help us understand the ongoing life and growth of the church? Paul answers this question in Ephesians 4:7–16. Central to Paul's teaching in this passage is the fact of Christ's ascension (Eph. 4:8–10). Just as God prophesied through David in Psalm 68, Christ is a victorious king who shares the spoils of His victory with His people. Therefore, Paul reasons, "grace was given to each one of us according to the measure of Christ's gift" (Eph. 4:7). In Ephesians 4:11, Paul enumerates the various gifts that Christ has supplied the church: "the apostles, the prophets, the evangelists, the shepherds and teachers." The common denominator among these gifts is the Word of God (see 1 Cor. 12:28). Each of these is a "Word gift." That is to say, Christ has given these gifts to the church in order to bring the Word of God to the church.[8] This great work, Paul is saying, is the fruit and evidence of Christ's glorious ascension. It will continue until Christ returns at the end of the age.[9]

To what end has Christ supplied the church with these Word gifts? Paul answers this question in the next verse: "to equip the saints for the work of ministry, for building up the body of Christ" (Eph. 4:12). Today, when ministers and elders in the church preach and teach the Word of God before

---

8  Of course, they do so in different ways. Apostles and prophets were used of God to bring new revelation to the church in the first century. The revelation that God opted to preserve in order to provide the norm for the faith and life of His new covenant people until the return of Christ is the New Testament. Because this revelation is complete and sufficient for faith and practice, the offices of Apostle and prophet are not continuing offices in the church. Apostles and prophets, rather, constitute the once-for-all foundation upon which the church now is being built (see Eph. 2:20). "Pastors and teachers" (likely a single office) refers to a continuing office in which men minister the Scriptures of the Old and New Testaments to the church until the return of Christ.

9  As we will see below, Christ's gifting of the church with "pastors and teachers" is in place until the church arrives at maturity (Eph. 4:13). Perfect maturity will not happen until Christ returns (Eph. 5:26–27). Therefore, we expect such officers to continue in the church until the consummation.

the church, they are preparing the people of God to undertake the work of serving one another, and they are edifying or building up the church.

What is the template of a maturing church? To what goal should the church aspire? Paul answers these questions in the following verse. The church aspires to "the unity of the faith and of the knowledge of the Son of God, to mature manhood, to the measure of the stature of the fullness of Christ" (Eph. 4:13). As with any maturing human being, the church also ought to aspire to be mature and not to remain in immaturity.

As Paul outlines them here, the marks of maturity are at least two—a common commitment to the teaching of Scripture and agreement about its meaning, and conformity to Jesus Christ. While Paul understands Christians to be receptive of the ministry of the Word, he does not understand them to be passive recipients. The Word received will equip them to detect and to distance themselves from error and deceit (Eph. 4:14). Furthermore, believers are to take the Word that they have received and, "speaking the truth in love," are to "grow up in every way into him who is the head, into Christ" (Eph. 4:15). So equipped by the ministry of the Word, we speak the Word to one another for our mutual profit. In that way, the church will grow up into Christ.

Putting these considerations together helps us see how Paul can say, on the one hand, that the body is engaged in its own growth ("Christ, from whom the whole body, joined and held together by every joint with which it is equipped, when each part is working properly, makes the body grow so that it builds itself up in love"; Eph. 4:15–16) and, on the other hand, that the church's growth comes from Christ ("the Head, from whom the whole body . . . grows with a growth that is from God"; Col. 2:19). The ascended Christ supplies the church with gifts. Chief among these gifts are Word gifts, that is, gifts by which people bring the Word of God to the church. Through such gifts, God's people are equipped, in the power of the Spirit of Christ, to serve one another. It is as God's people serve one another in this fashion that the whole body matures and grows. While the church's growth comes *through* believers' serving one another, that growth comes *from* Christ, the church's living Head.

## Qualifications for Elders

Those who minister the Word of God within the church today play a critical role in the church's ongoing growth. They are Christ's gifts to the church.

Understandably, Paul devotes considerable time and attention to spelling out their qualifications and job descriptions. In his Pastoral Epistles, and especially in 1 Timothy 3:1–7 and Titus 1:5–9, Paul details the qualifications of elders, that is, of those men who teach the Word and rule in the church.[10] These qualifications fall into two basic categories.

First, the elder must be doctrinally sound and capable of communicating sound doctrine. "He must hold firm to the trustworthy word as taught, so that he may be able to give instruction in sound doctrine and also to rebuke those who contradict it" (Titus 1:9). As such, the elder must be "able to teach" (1 Tim. 3:2). Even if he is not engaged in pulpit ministry, the elder should be able to explain Scripture's meaning to God's people in a way that is understandable and that promotes their edification.

Second, the overwhelming majority of Paul's qualifications for the eldership concerns the elder's life and character. Paul wants the church's elders to serve as examples to those who believe (1 Tim. 4:12), even as Paul himself lived to present himself as an example to the church (1 Cor. 11:1; Phil. 4:9; 2 Thess. 3:9; 1 Tim. 1:16).[11] Elders are to serve as examples to the flock in every department of life—"in speech, in conduct, in love, in faith, in purity" (1 Tim. 4:12).

Paul defines the job description of the elder when he tells Timothy, "What you have heard from me in the presence of many witnesses entrust to faithful men, who will be able to teach others also" (2 Tim. 2:2). Paul tells Timothy and, by extension, all ministers to devote themselves "to the public reading of Scripture, to exhortation, to teaching" (1 Tim. 4:13). The primary task of the elder is to read and teach the Scripture to the church. Elders are neither to add to nor to take away from the Scripture that has been entrusted to them. Coupled with this responsibility to teach the Scripture is the charge to tend the flock of God (see Acts 20:17–35). Elders are shepherds who must care for the spiritual needs of the sheep. They do so by the wise application of God's Word to the lives and circumstances of His people.

---

10 According to 1 Timothy 5:17, ministers are a type of elder whom the church financially supports to preach and teach the Word in a full-time capacity. While other elders (sometimes called "ruling elders" in the contemporary church) teach and rule alongside the minister, these elders do not serve the church in a full-time and remunerated fashion and typically do not engage in regular pulpit ministry.

11 Furthermore, believers have a calling to serve as examples to one another (1 Thess. 1:7).

## Lessons for Today

What lessons does Paul's teaching about the church have for us today? First, Paul insists that the Christian life be lived in the context of an acknowledged relationship with fellow believers who are committed to the worship of God and godly living. That is to say, Paul expects that every Christian will be a member of a local church. Private exercises of devotion are necessary, but they are not enough. We need to be with God's people for worship, service, and fellowship. Luke's account of Paul in Acts is that of a man who loved the church, who served the church, and who went out of his way to worship with and enjoy the fellowship of the church. Paul laid no burden on believers that he did not gladly and willingly bear himself.

Why is it so necessary that we be members of a local church? Paul has shown us that we need the ministry of the Word in the local church. We need the gifts of our fellow believers, even as they need our gifts. A host of the commands relating to Christian sanctification are the so-called "one another" commands, which assume an existing network of Christian relationships (for example, Eph. 4:2, 25, 32; 5:19, 21). The Christian life, therefore, must be lived in the context of godly relationships with the believers in the local church of which we are a part. For these reasons and more, membership and participation in the local church is a "must" of the Christian life.

Second, Paul's teaching on the church helps us see how important unity is in the church. Unity is both a fact and a command. We have seen Paul insist that we are now one in Christ. In light of that existing unity, we are bound to give expression to that unity, to "maintain the unity of the Spirit in the bond of peace" (Eph. 4:3). We obey that command precisely through our commitment to the truth of the gospel. The pattern that we observed in Ephesians 4:7–16 was that of a vibrant body united around the life-giving truth supplied by her Head, Jesus Christ. Sadly, many pit unity against the truth, as though unity requires sacrificing or compromising the truth. On the contrary, Paul insists, any form of unity that is accepting of error is no true unity at all. The united body of Christ exhibits unity as she "speak[s] the truth in love" to herself (Eph. 4:15). Truth is not an impediment to unity. It is the way that the church strives for and experiences her unity in Christ.

Third, Paul's teaching on the church reminds us that every believer has received some gift for the growth of the whole body. Some of the Corinthians fell prey to the temptation of using gifts to foster division and competition in the church and to nurture pride. The way that Paul checks that temptation is by reminding us of the nature and purpose of every spiritual gift. Because gifts come from God the Holy Spirit and are distributed according to His will, we have no cause for boasting (1 Cor. 4:7). Gifts are given for service, not self-indulgence. They are intended to build others up, not to tear them down. To be sure, certain gifts are "higher" than others, for reasons that we have seen (1 Cor. 12:31). But no gift, however spectacular, eminent, or fruitful in the church, puts one beyond the need of even the humblest gifts in the church. The question each of us must ask is, are we showing gratitude to the God who has graciously gifted us in Christ by using our gifts according to His mind and for His glory, and by receiving with gratitude the gifts of our brothers and sisters in Christ?

# Chapter 12

# PAUL AND THE FUTURE

Many have aptly described Paul's gospel along these lines: The future has broken into the present. In justification, the verdict of the last day has been pronounced upon the one who believes in Christ. The believer looks forward to the day of judgment knowing that he now stands righteous in Christ before a righteous God. In sanctification, believers by grace have begun to share in eternal glory: "We all, with unveiled face, beholding the glory of the Lord, are being transformed into the same image from one degree of glory to another. For this comes from the Lord who is the Spirit" (2 Cor. 3:18). Having tasted of this glory in part, we now "rejoice in hope of the glory of God" in full (Rom. 5:2).

For Paul, the Christian's future consists of the triune God's putting the finishing touches on His saving work, which has already begun in the Christian's present. We are not yet where we will be. As Romans 7 has reminded us, believers strive for a Christlikeness that they want but do not yet fully possess. The church as a whole, we have seen from Ephesians 4, is growing toward a maturity that she does not yet completely experience. Even so, the believer will most certainly be fully conformed to the image of Jesus Christ, and the church will most certainly attain "to mature manhood, to the measure of the stature of the fullness of Christ" (Eph. 4:13).

This future work is not disconnected from what God is doing in our lives right now. This future work will bring to completion what God has begun in the present: "I am sure of this, that he who began a good work in you will bring it to completion at the day of Jesus Christ" (Phil. 1:6). What every Christian anticipates in the future is organically related to what he has seen God do in his life in the past and in the present.

How, then, does Paul speak of this work that is yet to come? He does so in the broader context of discussing what God will do in relation to all people and to the world that He made. We may look at this work of God, comprehensively considered, by asking two questions. First, what is it that God has yet to do in the lives of individual human beings? Second, what is it that God has yet to do in the world?

## God's Future Work in Humans

What is it that God has yet to do in the lives of individual human beings? At least three lines of the Apostle's teaching inform our understanding of this work of God. First, there is what remains for the believer in the *intermediate state*. The phrase refers to the period of time between the believer's death and the return of Christ. It is possible, of course, that Christ may return before we die (see 1 Thess. 4:13–17), and it is our desire that Christ return soon (1 Cor. 16:22). Believers, however, should prepare to die before Christ's return. What happens to the believer at his death? What can be said of the believer during this interim period?

With the other biblical writers, Paul understands death to be the temporary separation of one's soul and one's body. He can describe death as being "away from the body" (2 Cor. 5:8). One's body is committed to burial, while the soul goes to be "at home with the Lord" (2 Cor. 5:8). As Paul puts it to the Philippians, "My desire is to depart and be with Christ" (Phil. 1:23). The soul of the believer, then, goes immediately upon death to be present with the Lord Jesus Christ, who now dwells in heaven (Phil. 3:20).

This state, Paul stresses, is unquestionably preferable to our present circumstances. Paul calls the Christian's death "gain" (Phil. 1:21) and describes being with Christ, upon and subsequent to the believer's death, as "far better" than continuing to live on earth (Phil. 1:23). This is a better situation because we will enjoy closer and richer fellowship and communion with Christ in glory. We will have left our mortal bodies (all the while, we will see, carrying the hope of an immortal body). In the presence of Christ, we will be freed from the presence of sin in our lives and from the influences of the world, the flesh, and the devil.

Our bodies, of course, undergo corruption ("this perishable body"; "this mortal body"; 1 Cor. 15:53). Even so, our bodies remain united to Christ. In explaining to the Thessalonian believers what will happen on the day of resurrection, Paul says that "the dead in Christ will rise first" (1 Thess. 4:16). Even though believers have died, they remain "in Christ." They remain united to Christ, soul and body, even though death has temporarily separated soul from body. The believer's body remains united to Christ even in the grave.

The second line of Paul's teaching about what God has yet to do in the lives of human beings concerns the future of unbelievers. Paul seldom reflects on the outcome and eternal state of the wicked. When he does, however, he paints a clear but fearful picture of things to come. On the day of judgment, Christ will raise all human beings from the grave. In his sermon to Felix, Paul speaks of "a resurrection of both the just and the unjust" (Acts 24:15). Unbelievers will be raised bodily, and they will live in those bodies forever.

So raised, unbelievers must appear before Jesus Christ as their vengeful Judge. Paul tells the Thessalonians that Jesus will appear "in flaming fire, inflicting vengeance on those who do not know God and on those who do not obey the gospel of our Lord Jesus" (2 Thess. 1:8). We have seen Paul teach in Romans 1 that all human beings by nature rebel against the God whom they know from the things that are made. They now abide under God's wrath, and they now experience a foretaste of eternal wrath to come. There are no innocents before the judgment seat of Christ.

As we have also seen, unbelievers will suffer a punishment that is both privative and positive. They will be deprived of the favorable glorious presence of Christ that the redeemed will enjoy for eternity; they will be "away from the presence of the Lord and from the glory of his might" (2 Thess. 1:9). Positively, they will "suffer the punishment of eternal destruction," that is, a destruction that always destroys and never ceases (2 Thess. 1:9). They will experience this as whole persons in their own resurrected bodies.

Although Paul does not explicitly discuss the intermediate state of unbelievers, we may presume that their souls enter into punishment and misery as they await the last judgment. We may also presume that their bodies are reserved in the grave for the resurrection on the last day, when the bodies that were instruments of sinning, now reunited with their sinful souls, will become vessels of God's just punishment for sin.

The third line of Paul's teaching about what God has yet to do in the lives of human beings concerns the future of believers at and after the glorious return of Christ at the end of the age.[1] When Christ returns, our perfectly holy souls will then be forever reunited with our resurrected bodies. Those bodies will be our bodies, but they will be thoroughly transformed. Paul helps us understand what our new bodies will be like by contrasting them with our present bodies: "So it is with the resurrection of the dead. What is sown is perishable; what is raised is imperishable. It is sown in dishonor; it is raised in glory. It is sown in weakness; it is raised in power. It is sown a natural body; it is raised a spiritual body" (1 Cor. 15:42–44). Paul here describes our present "natural" bodies as perishable, dishonorable, and weak. Our "spiritual" bodies will be imperishable, honorable, and characterized by power. In saying that our resurrection bodies are "spiritual," Paul does not mean that they will be immaterial. He means, rather, that they will be altogether transformed by, indwelt by, and controlled by the Holy Spirit. The Spirit who does this work is the same Spirit, of course, who now indwells our bodies. The Spirit presently works inwardly and secretly. There remains a work of the Spirit that will be outward, visible, and comparatively powerful.

What accounts for this character of our resurrection bodies? The brief answer, according to Paul, is that our bodies will take on the character of Christ's resurrection body. When Christ appears, Paul writes to the Philippians, Christ will "transform our lowly body to be like his glorious body, by the power that enables him even to subject all things to himself" (Phil.

---

1 Some believers have appealed to 1 Thessalonians 4:17 to say that Paul teaches a secret "rapture" of believers sometime between the present and Christ's return at the end of the age. This rapture is sometimes said to inaugurate a sequence of end-time events, including a millennial age, the rebuilding of the temple, and an earthly reign of Christ from Jerusalem. What Paul describes in 1 Thessalonians 4:17, however, is a description of the public, visible return of Christ at the end of the age and the ingathering of all believers to Christ at His return. The sole remaining event in redemptive history, according to Paul and the other New Testament writers, is Christ's return in glory. It is for this reason that Paul repeatedly urges believers to remain spiritually alert in anticipation of that day (Rom. 13:11–14; 1 Thess. 1:10; 5:1–10; 2 Thess. 1:5–12). To say this, however, does not mean that Paul did not anticipate signs or anticipations of that final day. Paul's teaching about the rise of the "man of lawlessness" in 2 Thessalonians 2 and a more expansive gospel work among ethnic Jews in Romans 11 are negative and positive harbingers, respectively, of that impending day.

3:21). The goal and outcome of our salvation is that we will be conformed—soul and body—to Christ.

We may here also appreciate once again the breadth and scope of the ministry of the Spirit. The Spirit by whom Jesus was raised from the dead and now indwells us is the same Spirit by whom our mortal bodies will be raised. Furthermore, what the Spirit did for the body of Jesus He will do for our bodies. The fact that Jesus has already been raised from the dead assures us that we, too, will undergo what Christ underwent at His resurrection. Jesus Christ is "the firstfruits of those who have fallen asleep," the beginning or first installment of the end-time resurrection harvest (1 Cor. 15:20).

What will happen to believers after their souls are reunited with their transformed bodies at the resurrection? First, Christ will gather them all to Himself. When Christ appears in glory, Paul tells the Colossians, "then you also will appear with him in glory" (Col. 3:4). This proximity or nearness of believers to Christ helps to explain Paul's declaration that "the saints will judge the world" and "judge angels" (1 Cor. 6:2–3). Believers will stand with Christ as He pronounces judgment on unbelieving people and reprobate angels.

Believers themselves will be judged by Christ, "For we must all appear before the judgment seat of Christ, so that each one may receive what is due for what he has done in the body, whether good or evil" (2 Cor. 5:10; see Rom. 14:10–11; 2 Tim. 4:1). Christ will judge all human beings, believing and unbelieving. But what about the believer's justification? If, through faith in Christ, the sinner is declared righteous before God, then what is the purpose of this judgment? If the end-time verdict has already been pronounced over us in Christ, why will we undergo judgment at the last day?

Paul does not teach that the believer's justification hangs in the balance on the day of judgment. Soon after the verse that we have just cited (2 Cor. 5:10), Paul gives one of the clearest statements in his correspondence of the justifying imputed righteousness of Christ (2 Cor. 5:21). Paul understands that when the believer stands before Christ's judgment seat at the last day, he stands as a justified person. He stands as one already counted righteous solely because of Christ's righteousness imputed to him. The fact that each believer is clothed in Christ's righteousness alone for his justification should provide comfort and assurance as we look ahead to the day of judgment. We possess the very righteousness of the Judge before whom we will stand, and our justification is a matter that has already been settled.

What, then, is the goal or purpose of this judgment if it is not to justify us? Christ's goal in this judgment is to evaluate our deeds. Paul speaks of the "reward" that Christ will give us "if the work that anyone has built on the foundation [which is Jesus Christ] survives" (1 Cor. 3:14; see 3:11). The reward is not something that we merit by our good works (1 Cor. 4:7). God is pleased, rather, freely to give this reward in proportion to our service to Christ. That there will be degrees of reward (1 Cor. 3:15) is an incentive to believers to "make it our aim to please him" by abounding in good works (2 Cor. 5:9).[2] It is also a disincentive to thinking and living in ways that will not meet with Christ's approval on the last day (1 Cor. 3:12–15).

What happens to believers after this judgment? Paul puts it pithily and pregnantly: "We will always be with the Lord" (1 Thess. 4:17). This eternal or everlasting presence with Christ will be in company with all His people ("*we* will always be with the Lord"). Having already begun to "reign in life," we will then experience consummately and to the fullness of our capacity that life. Having been granted glimpses of the glory of Christ (2 Cor. 3:18) and having hoped for more glory in this life (Rom. 5:2), we will then enter into what Paul calls "eternal glory" (2 Tim. 2:10).

This fullness of life and glory is a state of consummate and unbroken holiness. When Christ returns, we will all be "blameless in holiness" in the presence of God, a blamelessness that finds its root in our "hearts" (1 Thess. 3:13). Clothed in our resurrection bodies, we will no longer battle sin, and death will have been "swallowed up in victory" (1 Cor. 15:54; see v. 26).

Furthermore, when Christ returns, He will "[destroy] every rule and every authority and power" (1 Cor. 15:24). All the enemies of Christ, angelic and human, will be finally judged and committed to eternal punishment. At that moment, the Son will "[deliver] the kingdom to God the Father" (1 Cor. 15:24). With the subjection of "all things" to the Father, and the messianic Son's subjection of Himself to the Father, Christ's kingdom will have reached its appointed consummation. Then, God will be "all in all" (1 Cor. 15:28).

---

2   Although Paul does not tell us in so many terms what this "reward" is, it is reasonable to surmise that the "reward" involves degrees of the enjoyment of the life that is freely given in Christ. That is to say, a greater "reward" is a richer experience of communion and fellowship with Christ in glory than what one would otherwise have received.

To say that God will be "all in all" in no way removes or displaces Christ from the center of heavenly worship and praise. Paul's account of Christ's exaltation in Philippians 2:9–11 helps us see this point. Because Christ has been exalted and given "the name that is above every name," "every knee" will "bow" at "the name of Jesus" and "every tongue confess that Jesus Christ is Lord, to the glory of God the Father."[3] Significantly, that Christ is exalted in this fashion in no way detracts from the Father's glory. On the contrary, this adoration and worship of Christ redounds to the glory of the Father.

What will make our experience of worship and fellowship with God so rich is that our adoration of God will be in full knowledge of Him. In helping the Corinthians to get a proper perspective on the partial and provisional character of our present Christian experience, Paul writes that "now we see in a mirror dimly," but then our sight of God will be "face to face." Now we know Him "in part; then [we] shall know fully, even as [we] have been fully known" (1 Cor. 13:12). Our very best worship and fellowship with the triune God in the present is but a faint glimpse of what is yet to come.

If we were to choose one word that would capture the eternal state, it would be *glory*. As Paul concludes his exposition in Romans of the work of God in saving sinners by saying, "For from him and through him and to him are all things. To him be glory forever. Amen" (Rom. 11:36). The glory, or manifested excellence, of the triune God—Father, Son, and Spirit—will have filled our souls and transformed our bodies. It will characterize all of our experiences and activities in the eternal state. And the best part of all is that this glory will never cease. We will never weary of it, and our desire to commune with our God will be forever satisfied.

## Assurance of Salvation

Paul is well aware that these realities prompt a question in the minds of many believers: "I know that the eternal state will be wonderful beyond imagination, but how can I know whether I will be there?" Paul knows that believers may occasionally or chronically struggle with the assurance that they belong to Christ and will dwell with Him in glory forever.

---

3 Notably, every reasonable creature will acknowledge, in tongue and in posture, the lordship of Jesus Christ. Believers, of course, will do it willingly and gladly. Unbelievers will do it, but under external constraint and without delight.

One place in his letters where Paul helps believers rise to this assurance is Romans 8. As we have seen, this chapter follows on the heels of the grim realities portrayed in Romans 7. The believer is indwelt by the Spirit, and yet he struggles with the presence of remaining sin as well. The tension posed by this mutual indwelling comes to expression in Romans 7:14–25. Believers want to please God and obey His law. But believers are also beset, checked, deceived, and outmaneuvered by sin. We do not always do what we want, and we sometimes find ourselves doing what we do not want to do. We may well ask the question, will sin overcome me in the end? The fact that two other powerful and implacable opponents—the world and the devil—stand against us only compounds our dilemma. What assurance do we have that we will make it?

Paul elsewhere in his letters tells us *that* we will make it. "And I am sure of this, that he who began a good work in you will bring it to completion at the day of Jesus Christ" (Phil. 1:6). It is in Romans 8 that Paul helps us better to understand *how* and *why* we will make it. The Apostle arms us with arguments assuring us that true believers will persevere to the end.

We may identify at least three such arguments in Romans 8, each of which is centered on the activities of the three persons of the Godhead. First, there is the ongoing ministry of the indwelling Spirit. The Holy Spirit, we have seen in an earlier chapter, indwells every believer. He is not idle but is at work in us. We may point to at least three examples of the Spirit's activity in Romans 8. First, He enables us to put sin to death (Rom. 8:13). We have no power of our own to stand against sin. The Spirit, however, is able to assist us effectively to deal sin the mortal blow. Second, the Spirit "bears witness with our spirit that we are children of God" (v. 16). The Spirit, Paul says, conjoins His distinct witness to our own witness to our sonship. This witness of the Spirit is especially evident when we cry to God as our heavenly Father in our hour of need (v. 15). Because it is the Spirit's witness, we have infallible assurance that we are God's redeemed children. Third, the Spirit is pleased to "[help] us in our weakness" (v. 26). The Spirit does not despise us or abandon us in all our frailties and necessities, but He comes alongside us to aid us.[4] One symptom of our weakness is that "we do not

---

4  "Weakness" should not be taken to mean only those rare moments of helplessness and need that we experience in the Christian life. Paul uses this word in a variety of far-ranging ways. Paul has used

know what to pray for as we ought" (v. 26). The Spirit helps this deficiency of ours by "interced[ing] for us with groanings too deep for words" (v. 26). He "intercedes for the saints according to the will of God" (v. 27). We may be assured, then, that our prayers will be heard and accepted by the Father.

The second argument presented in Romans 8 for the assurance of the believer concerns the purpose of the Father. In the well-known verses of Romans 8:29–30, Paul outlines what has been called the Golden Chain of the believer's salvation: "For those whom he foreknew he also predestined to be conformed to the image of his Son, in order that he might be the first-born among many brothers. And those whom he predestined he also called, and those whom he called he also justified, and those whom he justified he also glorified." Paul is saying that those whom the Father has chosen from before the foundation of the world (see Eph. 1:4) will most certainly be called, justified, and ultimately glorified. No Christian is ever left behind. Paul conceives of no possibility that a predestined person will not be called, justified, and glorified. Why is this the case? It is because of the Father's purpose, which Paul has mentioned in the previous verse ("We know that for those who love God all things work together for good, for those who are called according to his purpose"; Rom. 8:28). It is the purpose of God that ensures that "all things work together for [our] good." It is the purpose of God that ensures that all those whom He has predestinated and called will arrive at consummate glory.

The third argument presented in Romans 8 for the assurance of the believer concerns the saving work of the Son. Christ has died, been raised, and now intercedes for us at the right hand of the Father in glory (Rom. 8:33–34). For this reason, we can never fall under condemnation ("Who is to condemn?"; v. 34), and no one or nothing can "separate us from the love of Christ" who purchased us with His own blood, rose from the dead for us, and now lives to intercede for us (v. 35).

---

a form of this word to describe believers prior to their conversion (Rom. 5:6) and to characterize the presence and influence of the "flesh" (Rom. 8:3). Paul can use this word of Christ at the cross (2 Cor. 13:4), to describe himself in his Apostolic labors (2 Cor. 11:30; 12:9), and to describe our present, mortal bodies (1 Cor. 15:43). In light of the many wide-ranging meanings that "weakness" can have in Paul's letters, Paul's statement in Romans 8:26 is best taken as comprehensive of our present existence as believers in this age. The Spirit's ministry, described here, is no less comprehensive. I owe this observation to Dr. Richard B. Gaffin Jr.

But neither can anything separate us "from the love of God in Christ Jesus our Lord" (Rom. 8:39). Paul wants us to understand that it is the love of the Father that provided for our salvation by sending Christ into the world. Paul reasons this way at verse 32: "He who did not spare his own Son but gave him up for us all, how will he not also with him graciously give us all things?" Surely He will give us all things, for, since "God is for us, who can be against us?" (v. 31). The Father has given us the greatest conceivable proof and demonstration of His own love for us—He did not spare His beloved Son, but gave Him up to the death of the cross. How, then, can we doubt His love for us all the way to the end?

Paul gives us these three arguments to encourage us to persevere in the Christian life. We face obstacles that are beyond our own power to overcome. But our God is with us. The Father, the Son, and the Spirit distinctly yet conjointly labor to bring us all the way to the glorious outcome of our salvation. Knowing these things, we labor on as "more than conquerors through him who loved us" (Rom. 8:37).

## God's Future Work in the World

We have thus far traced what Paul says about the future of the individual believer. That future, of course, is a future that is spent in the presence of Christ and in the midst of all His people. It is also a future that is not disembodied. It is a future that involves our glorified resurrection bodies. Just as Christ's body was raised gloriously by the Spirit, so also our bodies will be raised gloriously by the Spirit.

Our future, glorified existence, then, is both corporate and embodied. Paul shows us, furthermore, that there is a future for the created world in which we now live. In Romans 8, Paul helps us understand what that future is. Paul everywhere teaches that the good God made the world good (see 1 Cor. 8:6; 1 Tim. 4:4). The creation, however, "was subjected to futility" and now is in "bondage to corruption" (Rom. 8:20–21). The reason that the creation is in this present condition is not because God made the world this way. It is because "sin came into the world through one man, and death through sin" (Rom. 5:12). Therefore, the creation now "[groans] together in the pains of childbirth until now" (Rom. 8:22). But just as childbirth has a hoped-for outcome (the birth of a baby), so the creation's groanings have a hoped-for outcome. That hope is that "the creation itself will be set free from its bondage to corruption and obtain the freedom of the glory of the children of God" (Rom. 8:21). At the "redemption of our bodies," then, the creation will become a suitable habitation for the redeemed (Rom. 8:23). Glorified bodies will dwell in a world that is free from corruption and gloriously renewed at the return of Christ.

## Lessons for Today

What lessons does Paul's teaching about the future hold for believers today? First, Paul wants us to look to the future in hope and longing. He does not want us to dread the future. Neither does he want us to be so consumed with the present that we neglect what lies ahead for us as Christians. It is fair to say that Paul viewed his present from the vantage point of the future. It was this perspective, for instance, that enabled him to view suffering in its proper light (Rom. 8:17).

Paul chose to set these future realities before himself as a palpable "hope" that formed the subject of his meditations (Rom. 8:24–25). These future realities are not pious illusions or wishful thinking. They are, in fact, the completion or consummation in the lives of His people of what God has already begun for them in Christ. We hope and long for what is to come in the future precisely because we have been given a taste of it in the present. If we are to be living well for Christ in the present, we need to nurture a strong sense of our future hope. In order to do that, our minds need to be set on Christ and filled with the knowledge of what He has done, is doing, and will do for us in the power of the Spirit and according to the plan of the Father.

Second, our future hope is personal and individual, but it is not only that. Part of what is so attractive and enticing about the future is that it encompasses more than simply our souls and our bodies. We will dwell with Christ in the presence of all His people. Christ will present to Himself "the church . . . in splendor, without spot or wrinkle or any such thing, that she might be holy and without blemish" (Eph. 5:27). We will inhabit a world not in bondage to decay but renewed in glory. Of course, what we long for most is to be in the very presence of our Savior, whom we will worship in glory and splendor as we also worship the Father and the Spirit. Paul has no doubt that this is where history is advancing and will terminate. Do our lives—our worship, our relationships within and outside the church, our energies, our use of all the resources that God has given us—reflect these priorities right now?

> For from him and through him and to him are all things.
> To him be glory forever. Amen. (Rom. 11:36)

# ACKNOWLEDGMENTS

I am indebted to many people, without whose labors and assistance this book would not be in print. I am grateful to Ligonier Ministries for inviting me to film the video series that birthed *The Life and Theology of Paul.* Chris Larson kindly extended that invitation to me, and Dave Theriault labored professionally and heroically to see that series from conception to production to distribution. My teaching assistants, Nathan Lee and Luke B. Bert, read the manuscript, offering valuable suggestions and saving me from numerous gaffes and infelicities (any remaining blemishes are entirely my own). My editor at Reformation Trust, Kevin D. Gardner, carefully read the manuscript—his insightful editorial contributions surface throughout the book. The chancellor, Dr. J. Ligon Duncan III, and the Board of Trustees of Reformed Theological Seminary, and my colleagues on the Jackson campus have provided invaluable support, counsel, and assistance in my professional labors at RTS and in the church. My father, who passed away as this project was entering its final stages, and my mother have been pillars of support and love. My wife, Sarah, and our children, Phoebe, Lydia, and Thomas, have provided more love and encouragement than I could ever ask for or expect. Above all, I would trace these various streams to their one source, the triune God of heaven and earth. To Him alone I give supreme thanks, praise, and glory.

# SELECTED BIBLIOGRAPHY

Listed below are some additional resources for understanding the life and theology of Paul. While these titles do not by any means exhaust Paul's teaching, they are helpful as further reading for the curious student who desires to appreciate better the unique contributions that the Apostle to the Gentiles has made to our understanding of God and the Christian life. I have listed several titles by Sinclair B. Ferguson; while none of them deals specifically with Paul's theology, each of them is an able guide to that theology. Among my other contributions listed below, I also authored the chapters on Romans, 1–2 Corinthians, Galatians, and Ephesians in Dr. Michael J. Kruger's *A Biblical-Theological Introduction to the New Testament*.

Ferguson, Sinclair B. *By Grace Alone: How the Grace of God Amazes Me*. Orlando, FL: Reformation Trust, 2010.

———. *Devoted to God: Blueprints for Sanctification*. Edinburgh, Scotland: Banner of Truth, 2016.

———. *In Christ Alone: Living the Gospel Centered Life*. Orlando, FL: Reformation Trust, 2007.

———. *The Whole Christ: Legalism, Antinomianism, and Gospel Assurance; Why the Marrow Controversy Still Matters*. Wheaton, Ill.: Crossway, 2016.

Gaffin, Richard B. *By Faith, Not by Sight: Paul and the Order of Salvation*. 2nd ed. Phillipsburg, N.J.: P&R, 2013.

Kruger, Michael J., ed. *A Biblical-Theological Introduction to the New Testament*. Wheaton, Ill.: Crossway, 2016.

McRay, John. *Paul: His Life and Teaching*. Grand Rapids, Mich.: Baker Academic, 2007.

Murray, John. *The Epistle to the Romans*. Grand Rapids, Mich.: Eerdmans, 1960.

Ridderbos, Herman. *Paul: An Outline of His Theology*. Grand Rapids, Mich.: Eerdmans, 1997.

Vos, Geerhardus. *The Pauline Eschatology*. Phillipsburg, N.J.: P&R, 1979.

Waters, Guy Prentiss. *A Christian's Pocket Guide to Justification: Being Made Right with God?* Fearn, Ross-shire, Scotland: Christian Focus, 2010.

———. *Justification and the New Perspectives on Paul: A Review and Response*. Phillipsburg, N.J.: P&R, 2004.

# SCRIPTURE INDEX

# SCRIPTURE INDEX

# ABOUT THE AUTHOR

**Dr. Guy Prentiss Waters** is the James M. Baird Jr. Professor of New Testament at Reformed Theological Seminary in Jackson, Miss. Before coming to RTS in 2007, he served as assistant professor of biblical studies at Belhaven University in Jackson. Dr. Waters is a graduate of the University of Pennsylvania (B.A.), Westminster Theological Seminary (M.Div.), and Duke University (Ph.D.). He is a teaching elder in the Presbytery of the Mississippi Valley (PCA). He is author or editor of several books, including *How Jesus Runs the Church, Justification and the New Perspectives on Paul,* and *The Federal Vision and Covenant Theology,* and has written dozens of chapters, articles, and reviews. He and his family reside in Madison, Miss.